100 WAL Buckinghamshire and Hertfordshire

compiled by

GEOFF SPRECKLEY

The Crowood Press

First published in 1998 by
The Crowood Press Ltd
Ramsbury
Marlborough
Wiltshire SN8 2HR

British Library Cataloguing-in-Publication Data
A catalogue record for this book is
available from the British Library

ISBN 1 86126 102 0

All maps by Janet Powell

Typeset by Carreg Limited, Ross-on-Wye, Herefordshire

Printed and bound in Great Britain by Biddles Ltd, Guildford and King's Lynn

CONTENTS

34.	Wareside	4m	(6km)
35.	Whaddon	4m	(6km)
36.	Weston	4m	(6km)
37.	Marsworth	4m	($6^1/_2$km)
38.	... and longer version	$8^1/_2$m	($13^1/_2$km)
39.	Piddington	4m	($6^1/_2$km)
40.	Burnham Beeches	$4^1/_2$m	(7km)
41.	Twyford	$4^1/_2$m	(7km)
42.	Hyde Heath	$4^1/_2$m	(7km)
43.	Great Missenden	$4^1/_2$m	(7km)
44.	Medmenham	$4^1/_2$m	(7km)
45.	Buckland Common	$4^1/_2$m	(7km)
46.	Stoke Mandeville	$4^1/_2$m	(7km)
47.	Great Offley	$4^1/_2$m	(7km)
48.	Langley	$4^1/_2$m	(7km)
49.	... and longer version	6m	(9km)
50.	Ivinghoe	$4^1/_2$m	(7km)
51.	... and longer version	9m	(14km)
52.	West Wycombe and Bradenham	$4^1/_2$m	(8km)
53.	Quainton	5m	($7^1/_2$km)
54.	Newland Park	5m	($7^1/_2$km)
55.	Denham	5m	($7^1/_2$km)
56.	Bourne End	5m	(8km)
57.	Little Missenden	5m	(8km)
58.	Stokenchurch	5m	(8km)
59.	Coombe Hill	5m	(8km)
60.	Wooburn Green	5m	(8km)
61.	Stone	5m	(8km)
62.	... and longer version	7m	(11km)
63.	Much Hadham	5m	(8km)
64.	Thornborough	5m	(8km)
65.	Bayford	5m	(8km)
66.	Essendon	5m	(8km)
67.	Stewkley	5m	(8km)
68.	Stoke Hammond	5m	(8km)
69.	... and longer version	8m	(13km)
70.	East Claydon	5m	(8km)

71.	Furneux Pelham	5m	(8km)
72.	Sandon	$5^1/_2$m	(8km)
73.	Beaconsfield	$5^1/_2$m	(8km)
74.	… and longer version	$7^1/_2$m	(11km)
75.	Long Crendon	$5^1/_2$m	(8km)
76.	Chandlers Cross	$5^1/_2$m	(8km)
77.	Sarratt	$5^1/_2$m	($8^1/_2$km)
78.	Hambleden	$5^1/_2$m	(9km)
79.	Bledlow	6m	(8km)
80.	Hill End and the Grand Union	6m	(9km)
81.	Walkern	6m	(9km)
82.	Bovingdon	6m	(9km)
83.	Tingewick	6m	(9km)
84.	Hardwick	6m	(9km)
85.	Berkhamsted	6m	(9km)
86.	Great Hampden	6m	($9^1/_2$km)
87.	Old Amersham	6m	($9^1/_2$km)
88.	Northaw	6m	($9^1/_2$km)
89.	Lacey Green	6m	(10km)
90.	Flaunden	6m	(10km)
91.	Nash	6m	(10km)
92.	Marlow	$6^1/_2$m	(10km)
93.	Waddesdon	$6^1/_2$m	(10km)
94.	Old Beaconsfield	$6^1/_2$m	(10km)
95.	Hertingfordbury	$6^1/_2$m	(10km)
96.	Ayot St Lawrence	$6^1/_2$m	(10km)
97.	Cublington	7m	(11km)
98.	The Aylesbury Arm	$7^1/_2$m	(11km)
99.	Chess Valley	8m	(13km)
100.	Kings Langley	10m	(16km)

PUBLISHER'S NOTE

We very much hope that you enjoy the routes presented in this book, which has been compiled with the aim of allowing you to explore the area in the best possible way - on foot.

We strongly recommend that you take the relevant map for the area, and for this reason we list the appropriate Ordnance Survey maps for each route. Whilst the details and descriptions given for each walk were accurate at time of writing, the countryside is constantly changing, and a map will be essential if, for any reason, you are unable to follow the given route. It is good practice to carry a map and use it so that you are always aware of your exact location.

We cannot be held responsible if some of the details in the route descriptions are found to be inaccurate, but should be grateful if walkers would advise us of any major alterations. Please note that whenever you are walking in the countryside you are on somebody else's land, and we must stress that you should *always* keep to established rights of way, and *never* cross fences, hedges or other boundaries unless there is a clear crossing point.

Remember the country code:

Enjoy the country and respect its life and work
Guard against all risk of fire
Fasten all gates
Keep dogs under close control
Keep to public footpaths across all farmland
Use gates and stiles to cross field boundaries
Leave all livestock, machinery and crops alone
Take your litter home
Help to keep all water clean
Protect wildlife, plants and trees
Make no unnecessary noise

The walks are listed by length - from approximately 1 to 10 miles - but the amount of time taken will depend on the fitness of the walkers and the time spent exploring any points of interest along the way. Nearly all the walks are circular and most offer recommendations for refreshments.

Good walking.

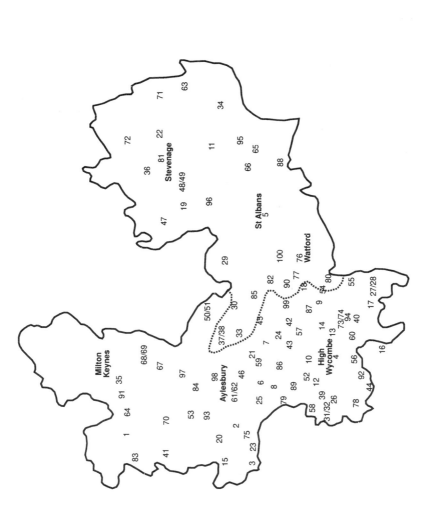

Milton
Keynes

Aylesbury

Stevenage

St Albans

Watford

High
Wycombe

1
83
41
64
91
35
70
53
93
2
75
20
23
3
15
97
84
98
61/62
46
25
6
8
89
79
58
31/32
26
39
52
12
10
56
92
44
78
67
68/69
59
21
86
24
43
57
13
4
60
14
73/74
94
40
16
37/38
33
7
42
99
87
9
55
17
27/28
50/51
30
85
82
90
77
76
100
29
47
19
96
5
88
66
65
95
11
34
36
81
48/49
72
22
71
63

Walk 1   **BUCKINGHAM** $1\frac{1}{2}$m (2km)

Maps: OS Sheets Landranger 165; Pathfinder 1046. Town Maps from the Tourist Information Office.

A short walk around this historic town.

Start: At 698342, the Tourist Information Office, Buckingham.

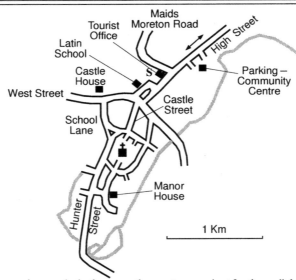

There are several car parks in the town, the most convenient for the walk being behind the Community Centre. Facing the Tourist Information Office, once known as the Old Gaol, keep left and cross Maids Moreton Road. Continue down High Street's north side. There are several interesting houses here, in an area that once included the market place. The garage at the end of High Street stands on the site of the Town Wharf at the end of the Buckingham Arm of the Grand Union Canal. Continue ahead into the new apartment development to find the Cannon, removed from Cannon Corner by the Old Town Hall, to protect it from the heavy traffic. Retrace your steps along the south side of the High Street, passing the Grand Junction Inn, another reminder of the canal. As you look up High Street, the Old Town Hall is ahead, a Georgian building, its clock surmounted by the gilded swan weather vane. In front of the Town Hall, to the left, is the White Hart Hotel with its early Victorian front. Pass in front of the

8

Town Hall and, with Castle Street on your left, continue along West Street. Look to the right, down Market Hill, to see the **Chantry Chapel**, the oldest building in Buckingham. On the corner of Market Hill is the Cobham Arms, a former coaching inn. The archway which would have given access to London-bound coaches. On the right, opposite School Lane, is **Castle House**. Go up School Lane, passing, on the right, the original infants school, now being converted into private residences. Bear left up Bristle Hill. One of the shop fronts on the left displays a large ammonite, said to have been dug out of a local sand pit. At the top, look down Castle Street to the **Villiers Hotel**. Turn right, passing the Coach House, on the right, to reach the Parish Church. Go around the left side of the church and down Church Street, passing some 16th- and 17th-century houses. On the corner is the former Congregational Church, now the Radcliffe Centre, part of Buckingham University. To the right is St Rumbold's Lane: on the corner of No. 7 is an example of quatrefoil carving of pre-Reformation date. Continue along Church Street, passing the site of the old hospital, founded in 1431 by John Barton. To the left is Twisted Chimney House. On this house is a plaque to St Rumbold, the 'baby saint' of Buckinghamshire. Bear right along a path through the old churchyard. To the right is the early Georgian Yeomanry House, restored by the University. Go down Hunter Street to the bridge over the River Ouse. Turn left before the railway bridge and then sharp left along a path beside the river. Cross the river, go through a parking area and cross a second footbridge into Chandos Park. Turn left along a tarmac path. Turn right, and then left, by the New Inn, into Bridge Street. Turn right before the bridge, passing the sadly derelict swimming pool. Turn left at the footbridge to return to the start.

POINTS OF INTEREST:
Chantry Chapel – At the Reformation, this Norman building ceased to be a chapel and became St John's Royal Latin School, which continued until 1907. The adjoining Masters House was rebuilt in 1690.

Castle House – The front facing the street was built in Queen Anne's time, but the west side is older. Among the famous people to have stayed here were Catherine of Aragon in 1513 and Charles I in 1644.

Villiers Hotel – Destroyed by fire in 1725, but rebuilt and renamed. Oliver Cromwell is said to have held a council of war in the Cromwell Room.

Twisted Chimney House – It is said that Elizabeth I once dined in this early Tudor Manor House.

REFRESHMENTS:
The walker is spoilt for choice in Buckingham.

Walk 2   **CUDDINGTON**   2m (3$\frac{1}{2}$km)

Maps: OS Sheets Landranger 165; Explorer 2.

A visit to one of Buckinghamshire's prettiest villages.

Start: At 738112, St Nicholas Church, Cuddington.

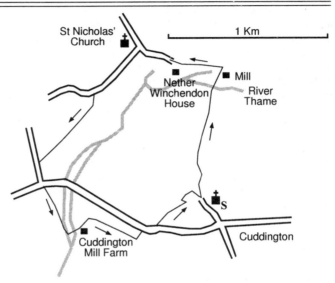

There is limited street parking in **Cuddington** - please park considerately. Walk down the lane with the church on your right, passing the village school. Where the lane bears right at Tyringham Hall, take the footpath along Tibbys' Lane. Go downhill, then bear right at a white, thatched cottage. Take the left fork to go over a footbridge and go through a gate into a field. Keep the hedge on your right as you follow the course of a small stream. Go over a stile and along a fenced path to reach a double stile. Go over and maintain direction to cross a footbridge over the River Thame. Now cross a stile by a metal gate, continuing to the Old Mill. Follow the gravel track to the left to go under the electricity wires, then ignore a stile on the right, continuing along a tarmac track. Follow an S-bend, with Nether Winchendon House on the left, to reach a road in **Nether Winchendon** outside St Nicholas' Church. Bear left at an unusual Victorian pillar box, in the middle of a grass triangle and, after a further 100 yards, turn left, on to a path signed as the Thame Valley Walk.

Bear left and head for the corner of bushes and then a stile to the left of a prominent tree in the hedge. Cross on to a road. Turn left and, after 100 yards, at a junction, go through the metal gate opposite and continue along the Thame Valley Walk. Bear left towards a gate. Beyond, cross a footbridge and go through two gates into the gardens of Cuddington Mill. Pass the house on your left, cross a patio and bear slightly right, looking for a pair of wooden doors with a public footpath sign. Go through the doors on to a road and turn left between Cuddington Mill and Cuddington Mill Farm. At the meeting of the drives of these two properties, turn right through a metal gate into a field and head to the right of the cottages. Cross a stile in the field corner and turn left, to cross another stile on to a road. Turn right and, after 15 yards, turn left along a signed footpath, heading for Cuddington church. At a pair of telegraph poles, continue ahead, walking beside the attractive rear gardens of several properties. Keep left of a large conifer to reach a kissing gate. Go through, cross a footbridge and retrace your outward steps to the church.

POINTS OF INTEREST:

Cuddington – The ochre-washed cottages around a village green make an ideal setting for one of the prettiest villages in Buckinghamshire. It is not surprising to learn that since 1985, when the village won the Wilkinson Sword for the Best Kept Village, it has been there or thereabouts on every succeeding year. Many years ago Cuddington was an important village for the making of lace. It was not a profitable trade for the local workers however: in 1867 a girl had to be pretty good if she was to earn two shillings a week.

St Nicholas' Church is Norman in origin, but has acquired a blend of many styles following substantial restoration over the years. It was Victorianised by George Street in 1857. Interesting items include an original Norman font, quaint epitaphs, the angels depicted in two 15th-century stained glass windows and the altar rail, which has a carving of a muzzled bear on one of its posts.

Nether Winchendon – The village is mentioned in the Domesday Book and for many years belonged to the Augustinian monks at nearby Notley Abbey. The church clock was installed in 1772, a gift from the Lady of the Manor – Mrs Jane Beresford – and is unique in that it has only one hand. Nether Winchendon House is basically of 16th-century origin, but with a Gothic Screen added in 1800. It has been the home of the Spencer-Bernard family for over 400 years.

REFRESHMENTS:
The Crown Inn, Cuddington.

Walk 3   **ICKFORD** $2^1/_2$m (4km)

Maps: OS Sheets Landranger 165; Pathfinder 1093.

A short, level walk exploring the two small villages of Ickford and Worminghall.

Start: At 648076, the Rising Sun Inn, Ickford.

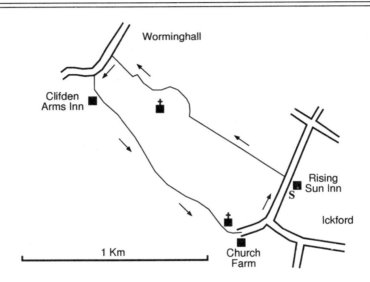

To reach the start, turn right off the A418 (Thame to Oxford) road. The inn has a reasonable car park - but check with the landlord before using it - and parking can also be found on some of the minor residential roads off the main street. Facing away from the Rising Sun, cross the road and take the signed footpath between houses to reach a stile into a field. Follow a path beside, initially, a wire fence and soon a fence and hedge on the right. Just before the right corner, cross a footbridge, keeping to the left edge of the next field. Cross another footbridge and follow a path on the left field edge, heading for some distant houses. Cross a stile in the corner on to a narrow path between houses and follow it to meet a wider tarmac drive. After ten yards, turn left through a wooden gate to reach a tarmac path, with the church of **St Peter and St Paul, Worminghall** on the left.

Follow the path through a series of kissing gates to reach a road by a mixture of old and new houses. Turn left along the road, passing the village shop. Now, where the main road turns right, bear left, down to the thatched, 16th-century Clifden Arms Inn. Keep to the left of the inn and go over a stile. Follow a concrete track initially, then a grass farm track. Go through a gate and a kissing gate, then leave the fence on the left, bearing right across a field to reach a footbridge below a single, obvious tree. Cross the bridge and the corner of the field beyond to a stile, then walk with a wire fence on your left. On reaching a lone chestnut tree, bear right, across the field, heading for **St Nicholas' Church, Ickford** . The next stile is directly below the church. Cross it and follow a path to a footbridge. Cross into the churchyard and follow the path to the right of the church leaving through the church gate. Continue ahead along a lane to reach the main village street. Turn left to return to the Rising Sun.

POINTS OF INTEREST:

St Peter and St Paul Church, Worminghall – The church is unusual in that it stands alone in a field approached over a cattle grid. It is a mixture of 12th- ,13th- and 14th-century styles, but was substantially restored and repaired in the 19th century, mainly financed by the family of Lord Clifden who lived in the Manor House. The black and white 16th-century village inn - the Clifden Arms - is a focal point of the village, hosting the village fete on a date as close as possible to the feast of St Peter and St Paul.

St Nicholas' Church, Ickford – The first church on this site was probably Saxon, though the oldest parts of the present building (the chancel, the centre aisle and nave, together with the lower part of the tower) date from the 12th century. The church escaped major 19th-century restoration and was sensitively repaired in the early part of the 20th century by Mr. Oldrid Scott who managed to retain many of the special earlier features. The pulpit and some of the pews are 17th-century, but much of the woodwork was by Canon Staley, completed between 1911 and 1933. Gilbert Sheldon, who was Rector of Ickford, became Archbishop of Canterbury, a position he held from 1663 to 1677.

REFRESHMENTS:
The Clifden Arms, Worminghall.
The Rising Sun, Ickford.

Maps: OS Sheets Landranger 175; Explorer 3.

A town walk, taking in some of High Wycombe's historic points.
Start: At 866931, High Wycombe Tourist Information Office.

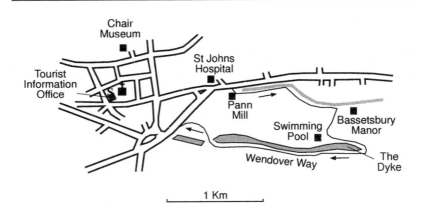

Turn left into the High Street, passing the Little Market House and its list of market tolls, as applicable in 1874, and mileages to London and Oxford above the two side arches. Continue along the High Street noting the **Red Lion** statue on the portico above Woolworths. Between the Red Lion and Lloyds Bank is a pair of shops, originally the home of the Wycombe Military Academy. This organisation was of great importance, being eventually transferred to Sandhurst for the training of junior officers. Cross the road to the brick and flint house (No. 30), at one time the home of Tom Burt, who has a hill named after him to the south of Wycombe. Retrace your steps along the High Street passing the Hobgoblin Inn, one of only two hostelries remaining on the main street. The second – The Falcon – is reached just before the **Guildhall**, at one time an important coaching inn, was destroyed by fire and has recently been restored and reopened. At the Guildhall, turn right up Church Street, then bear right through the churchyard of **All Saints' Church**. Bear right at the road to go up a path by the camera shop. Cross the railway and turn right: on the left is the **Wycombe Local History and Chair Museum**. On leaving the museum, turn left and then right over the railway into Crendon Street. The building you see ahead is Wycombe Abbey School, a public school for girls. Turn left into Easton Street at the lights, passing a brick and flint building (No. 17) which still bears the coat of arms from its previous use as the town Post Office. Continue for about 150 yards to reach the ruins of the Hospital of St John the Baptist on the left.

Continue for a few yards, then cross the road, soon passing Pann Mill, an old corn mill mentioned in the Domesday Book, on the right. The area ahead is some 47 acres of parkland known as 'The Rye'. Cross the bridge over the River Wye and turn left along a tarmac path through a children's playground. At a T-junction, turn right towards the open-air swimming pool. On the far left you can seen Bassetsbury Manor. Go past the swimming pool and, on reaching 'The Dyke', turn left to reach a small waterfall. Cross to the back of the Dyke and turn right towards the town. You are now following Wendover Way, a tree-lined walk named after Lord Wendover, the only son of the Marquis of Lansdown, who was killed in the 1914-18 War. At the end of Wendover Way there is a boathouse: continue ahead along the concrete track, soon bearing left along a footpath. Use the subway under the main road to reach Queen Victoria Road. Cross the bridge over the River Wye, go past the Town Hall and Library on the left and turn left at the lights to regain the High Street. Now reverse the outward route back to the start.

POINTS OF INTEREST:
Red Lion – The portico has seen many notable events. Benjamin Disraeli campaigned from here to become an MP (unsuccessfully in 1832) and Winston Churchill rallied support from here in the post-war election of 1946 (equally unsuccessfully).
Guildhall – Designed by Henry Keene and built in 1757, the hall was a gift from the Earl of Shelbourne. It was renovated in 1859. The old ceremony of Mayor Making is performed every year at the Guildhall. After the election of the new Mayor, the outgoing mayor is weighed. If he has gained weight during his year in office, it is considered that he has lived too well on ratepayers money and is jeered accordingly.
All Saints' Church – Founded in Norman times and consecrated by the Bishop of Worcester (1062-1095), the church was extended in 1275. It originally had a central tower, but this was removed in 1505. The Victorian restoration in 1887 was carried out, as at many local churches, by Oldrid Scott.
Wycombe Local History and Chair Museum – The museum is housed in a lovely brick and flint, 17th-century residence surrounded by splendid gardens. It has a large collection of woodworking tools and chairs illustrating the history of the furniture industry in the Chilterns. It is open from Monday to Saturday throughout the year.

REFRESHMENTS:
There are possibilities to suit all tastes and pockets in High Wycombe.

Walk 5   ST ALBANS $2\frac{1}{2}$m (4km)

Maps: OS Sheets Landranger 166; Pathfinder 1119.

A town walk giving a brief insight into historic St Albans.

Start: At 147073, the Town Hall, St Peter's Street, St Albans.

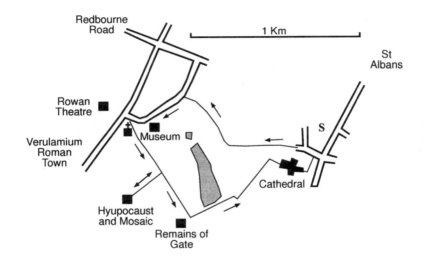

Facing the Town Hall, bear right down Market Place. The **Abbey** tower can be seen ahead. Keep right of the 17th-century Gables and go down French Row, passing the Fleur de Lys, an old inn. Turn right into High Street, passing to the left of the Tudor Tavern and going along George Street. The old Kings Arms and adjacent shop were built in the 1850s. Go through an area known as Romeland, going down Romeland Hill. Go past the Great Gate, on the left, and Romeland House, now an office block, on the right. Continue to Fishpool Street, named for a Saxon fishpond. Many of the buildings here are timber-framed with later brick fronts. No. 13 Fishpool Street was originally the Crow Inn, built in 1550: note the wide entrance to the former inn yard and the ornate plaster work on the overhang. Between Nos. 50 and 52, can be seen a war memorial plaque, for those who died in the 1914-18 war. The fine St Michael's Manor Hotel is now passed on the left. The oldest part of the building dates from the 16th century, the street elevation being 17th-century and the Doric columns on the side enclosing a 19th-century porch. Go past the Blue Anchor, another 16th-century timber-framed building , then bear left and, just before crossing the river, an example of Hertfordshire puddingstone can be seen in front of the 18th-century Kingsbury Water Mill Museum. The Museum still contains some of the original mill machinery. Cross the bridge over the River Ver into St Michael's Street, where there are more timber-framed buildings with later brick fronts. Go past the Rose and Crown Inn and enter the old Roman city of Verulamium. The Six Bells on the right is built over the site of a Roman baths dating from 60AD. Go past Darrowfield House, built in 1725, on the left, and bear left at the school to visit the Verulamium Museum.

Return to the main road, bearing left at the school into St Michael's Street. Cross the busy main road, with care, to view the **Roman Theatre**. Return to the main road, turn right, cross and go through the gates to the churchyard. Leave the churchyard and turn right in front of the Museum, where the remains of the basilica can be seen. Go through a car park into its top right corner and follow a sign to the Hypocaust. Cross the park and go through a line of trees to a low brick building. Here are the remains of a town house bath suite and its under floor heating or hypocaust. Turn right from the exit and, at the furthest line of trees, you can see the wall and foundations of the London Gate. Turn back towards the Abbey, keeping the lake on your left. Turn right past the Fighting Cocks and follow a footpath uphill towards the Abbey. Leave the Abbey by the south door and turn left through the yard to reach Holywell Hill. Now, facing the White Hart, turn left, cross at the traffic lights into Chequer Street and continue to St Peter's Street to return to the start.

POINTS OF INTEREST:

St Albans Abbey – The original Abbey was founded in 792 by Offa of Mercia, though nothing remains of that building. The present Abbey was built in 1077-88, shortly after the Norman Conquest. The Norman builders made use of the bricks taken from the ruins of Verulamium. The Abbey church only became a cathedral in 1877, though its head was made the premier Abbot of England in 1154.

Roman Theatre – This is one of the most important remains of the Roman city, the only fully-excavated theatre of the period in Britain. Built in approximately 150AD, it is one of only six theatres in Roman Britain. Dramatic productions and religious rites would have been seen here rather than gladiatorial contests. The theatre is open seven days a week throughout the year.

REFRESHMENTS:
Opportunities are many and varied around the town.

Walk 6   **GREAT KIMBLE**   3m (4$\frac{1}{2}$km)

Maps: OS Sheets Landranger 165; Explorer 2.

Level field paths beneath the steep scarp slope of the Chilterns.

Start: At 826058, in the slip road on the right, just before Great Kimble church on the A4010.

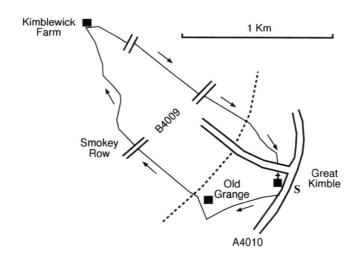

Parking is available beside 'Cymbeline' cottage, opposite the bus lay-by. Cross the road, with care, and follow the footpath, part of the **North Bucks Way**, towards the far field corner and the farm buildings. The Old Grange, with the remains of a moated site and a new stable block, is to your right. Cross a stile and the gravel drive to the Old Grange, and pass to the right of the summer house to cross another stile. Cross a paddock and, in the corner, turn right over a stile, keeping to the right edge of the large field beyond. Go over a stile and bear left to cross two stiles and the railway line. Continue ahead to reach a road by pretty thatched Clematis Cottage and join a tarmac drive. After some 30 yards, where the farm drive bears left, continue ahead along the North Bucks Way, now following a bridleway between hedges. Bear right at a metal gate and, after 100 yards, by a prominent tree in the hedge on your right, leave the North Bucks Way, taking a path on the left and crossing a stile by a metal gate. Bear half-right across a field to reach a stile to the right of a bushy tree. Cross this and, immediately, another stile, crossing the farm drive. Go through a metal gate into a small paddock and through another metal gate on the right of the hedge. Bear right across a field to a stile in the hedge, midway between a pair of white gates and a large, fenced-in tree. Cross the double stile and a footbridge, then turn right along a gravel drive going through white gates and over a cattle grid. Follow the tarmac path to a road. Cross the road and the stile opposite, and follow the right field edge. Beyond the last bungalow the path crosses the centre of the field to join a hedge.

With the hedge on your left, continue to reach a stile on to a road. Cross and go through the gap in the trees to a stile. Cross this and the field beyond to reach a stile in the corner. Cross and maintain direction, walking with the hedge on your right to reach a kissing gate in the corner. Go through, down steps, cross the railway line, with care, and go up the steps to reach a stile. Go through a hedge gap, cross a stream and go over a stile. Bear right in the next paddock, with a lily pond on your left, heading for the white waymarker arrow on a tree. Cross the stile behind the tree and bear right to pass Great Kimble School. Go through a metal gate, with the playground on the right, and cross a stile on to a short tarmac drive. Follow this to a road (Church Lane). Turn left by some pretty brick and flint cottages, with an old well in front of Moss Cottage and walk to **St Nicholas' Church, Great Kimble**. At the main road, turn right, the Bernard Arms is to your left, then cross, with care, to return to the start.

POINTS OF INTEREST:
North Buckinghamshire Way – The Way was set up by the Ramblers Association in 1972. It is about 35 miles long and runs from the Ridgeway National Trail near Wendover to the county boundary at Northampton.
St Nicholas' Church, Great Kimble – The church is famed as the place where John Hampden took his stand against the Ship Tax in 1637. The legend describes how he galloped up the hill and into the church to make his protest to the assembled tenants. The interesting and unusual hanging sign tells the story and a facsimile of the protest document can be seen inside. The village name, Kimble, derives from the British king Cunabelin or Cymbeline.

REFRESHMENTS:
The Bernard Arms, Great Kimble.

Walk 7   **SWAN BOTTOM**   3m (4¹/₂km)

Maps: OS Sheets Landranger 165; Explorer 2.

An easy, level, short walk mainly on woodland paths in the heart of the Chilterns.

Start: At 902055, the Old Swan Inn at Swan Bottom.

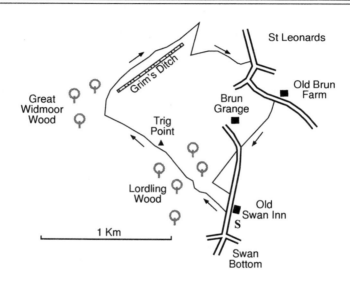

Swan Bottom is to the north of Great Missenden on the road through Hunt's Green and The Lee. Parking is available in the area opposite the inn. Facing the **Old Swan Inn**, take the gravel path between the inn and the houses. Ignore a footpath to the left and continue along the bridleway, heading for Lordling Wood. Ignore another path on the left, entering the wood along the track between the white house and a garage. Turn right, leaving the bridleway, then bear left along the wide path ahead, going through a stand of tall beech trees. At a crossing path, continue ahead, with a new plantation on your left, soon entering Great Widmoor Wood. Now keep to the main path, soon passing a trig. point (761 ft − 232m − above sea level). At the next crossing path, just before the main track bears left, turn right along a narrow, waymarked path.

On joining a wider path, turn left, and then immediately right along a narrow path into the centre of the wood. Go between brick pillars and bear left. Now ignore a brick squeeze stile on the left, continuing along the meandering path through the wood.

On emerging from the wood, with a field in front of you, turn right along a wide track and, after 15 yards, turn left along a footpath waymarked by yellow arrows. At a waymarked crossing path, continue ahead, following a narrow path between young trees and conifers. You are now following the line of the ancient earthworks known as **Grim's Ditch**. Just before the next crossing path, take a sharp right turn on to a path joining from the right. At the next T-junction, turn left, soon crossing a stile beside a horse barrier. Now follow the right edge of a field to reach a road.

Turn right and immediately right again following the sign for The Lee and Great Missenden. Go uphill and, near the top, turn left down Arrewig Lane. Now, just before reaching Old Brun's Farm, turn right through a gap in the hedge and follow a path beside a wire fence on the left. Turn right in the field corner, following a path with a hedge on the left. Go through a gap in the hedge and maintain direction to cross a stile into a paddock. Go past a large house on the right - Brun Grange - then cross a stile, a paddock and another stile to reach a road. Cross the road and follow the footpath opposite, going diagonally left across a field to reach the corner of Lordling Wood. Turn immediately left by two wooden posts, go through some small trees and fields and continue through the rear gardens of Kingswood Cottages to reach a road. Turn right, soon reaching the start.

POINTS OF INTEREST:

The Old Swan Inn – This is a 16th-century coaching inn. Its present day charm is very much in keeping with its age - open fires, brassware and flagstone floors.

Grim's Ditch – The ditch is now believed to be Britain's largest relic of early man, although its purpose is still widely debated. Traces of the ditch can be seen on many walks in the Chilterns. The ditch has in turn been attributed to Saxons, being the boundary of lands captured by Cuthwulf in 571; to King Offa, to protect his kingdom - and he certainly did have land in the Chilterns; and to the Danes to prevent cattle rustling. It has also been suggested that it was even to prevent the spreading of fires. Recent work by the Hertfordshire Archaeological Trust has suggested that the ditch probably dates from the 4th century BC.

REFRESHMENTS:
The Old Swan, at the start.

Walk 8   **WHITELEAF**   3m (4¹/₂km)

Maps: OS Sheets Landranger 165; Explorer 3.

*An undulating walk passing the Whiteleaf Cross and with
extensive views across the Vale of Aylesbury.*

Start: At 823036, the Whiteleaf Hill picnic site car park.

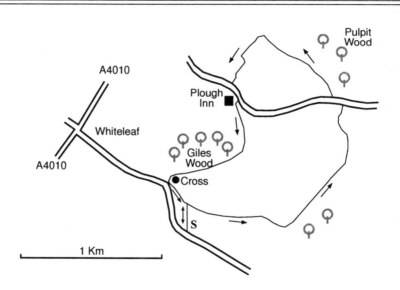

To reach the start, turn right off the Princes Risborough - Aylesbury Road (the A4010)
following the sign for Whiteleaf. The car park is on the left. Take the path in the top
left corner of the car park by the notice board and, on reaching a crossing path, turn
right along a track signed as a bridleway and marked with the **Ridgeway National
Trail** acorn symbol. After 100 yards, leave the track, turning right at a signpost to go
along a bridleway. Go through a wooden barrier and follow the track through the
trees along the edge of Hangings Wood. Bear right at a fork, following the bridleway
uphill. At a clearly waymarked crossing path, turn left to go downhill. Now ignore a
path joining from the left and continue ahead. Go over a track and, at a junction of
paths, continue basically ahead, remaining on the bridleway. Soon you go downhill
between wire fences - the path here can be very muddy after rain. Continue ahead at

a crossing path with Ninn Wood on your left. Soon the path narrows to join a gravel section and continues to a road. Cross the road and bear slightly left along a well-defined path, keeping to the right of a parking area. Go over a crossing path and through a barrier, passing a sign on the right depicting the layout of the Grangelands and Pulpit Hill Nature Reserve.

Continue ahead, going downhill with Pulpit Wood on your right. (On the summit of Pulpit Hill there is an Iron Age fort). At a joining of paths left and right, continue ahead along a bridleway, soon turning left through a wooden kissing gate and then bearing right, downhill. This area of natural chalk grassland is crossed by a multitude of paths. Basically you should head for the golf course on the hill in front of you, arriving at a kissing gate. Go through the gate and follow an undulating path to reach a barrier and, beyond, a road. Cross, turn left and, after 15 yards, take the slip road on the right, following it down to the Plough Inn. Just before the inn car park, turn right along the signed Ridgeway path, very soon bearing left at a fork and going through a kissing gate by a metal gate. Bear right at a fork, still following the Ridgeway acorn waymarkers. The path winds uphill into Giles Wood: continue ahead at a crossing path, still going quite steeply uphill. There are magnificent views from the top over the Vale of Aylesbury. Go through a kissing gate by the Whiteleaf Hill sign and ahead at the Ridgeway marker post to reach wooden railings and the **Whiteleaf Cross**. Return to the Ridgeway post and turn right to follow the National Trail, following the wide path to reach another Ridgeway sign. Here, bear left into the starting car park.

POINTS OF INTEREST:

Whiteleaf Cross – This cross, and its near neighbour the Bledlow, are the only two turf-cut crosses in Britain. Its origin is unclear, the most popular theory being that is was converted from an ancient fertility symbol. It is very hard to appreciate the size of the Cross from close to: it is much better seen from a distance. The Cross is on a 27 acre site over looking the scenic Chiltern scarp, with the Vale of Aylesbury beyond. The prominent position of Whiteleaf Hill with its ancient barrows, the Cross and the beech woodland make this area one of the most important sites within Buckinghamshire's Chilterns Area of Outstanding Natural Beauty (AONB).

Ridgeway National Trail – The Ridgeway is often referred to as 'the oldest green road in Europe'. The 85 mile Ridgeway National Trail, starting at Avebury and finishing at Ivinghoe Beacon, passes through five counties and two AONBs .

REFRESHMENTS:

The Plough, Lower Gadesden.
There is a wide and varied selection in nearby Princes Risborough.

Walk 9   **CHALFONT ST GILES**   3m (4$^1/_2$km)

Maps: OS Sheets Landranger 165 and 175; Explorer 3.

An easy, short walk along quiet lanes and field paths to the north-west of Chalfont St Giles. Milton's Cottage is a short diversion.

Start At: 990935, the Crown Inn, on the main street of Chalfont St Giles.

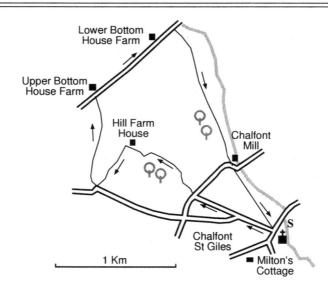

Take the road at the side of the inn (Up Corner) and continue uphill along Silver Hill, passing the Fox and Hounds Inn. At the fork, bear right down the attractive Dodds Lane. On reaching a crossroads, continue ahead down a rough track, Hill Farm Lane. Leave the houses, continuing ahead through a wood. Go past Hill Farm House and, at the cottages, turn right. Now, where the track bears to the right, bear left and then left again at a white marker post signed for Froghall. Cross a stile and keep to the right edge of the field beyond. Go through a kissing gate, and immediately turn right along a rough track.

Ignore two sets of stiles on the left, remaining on the track to pass Kiln Cottage. After a further 600 yards, ignore a path joining from the right and continue downhill to reach Upper Bottom House Farm. Turn right at the T-junction within the farm buildings and go down a narrow lane to pass Lower Bottom House Farm. After a further 200 yards, turn right along a path signed as part of the **South Bucks Way**, keeping to the left edge of a field. Cross a stile and maintain direction across the centre of the field beyond. Cross a stile into a small wood and continue along the left edge, ignoring paths to both left and right. You emerge from the wood along a narrow path with fields on either side: continue ahead, soon going along a rough track.

On reaching a lane, cross and continue ahead, passing the Old Mill on the left. After a further 50 yards, continue ahead along a gravel track which soon reverts to a narrow path. Ignore all turnings, remaining on this prominent path to reach a T-junction. There, turn left to return to the centre of **Chalfont St Giles**. **Milton's Cottage** lies along the main street to the west.

POINTS OF INTEREST:
South Bucks Way – This 23 mile long distance path links the Ridgeway National Trail at Coombe Hill, near Wendover, to the Grand Union Canal at Denham. The path follows the valley of the River Misbourne, one of only four rivers in the Chilterns, until it flows into the River Colne, and then meets the Grand Union towpath.
Chalfont St Giles – Despite being only 500 yards from a main road, Chalfont has preserved its identity as a charming village with a church, a pond, a village green and many old and pretty cottages. The church, found through an archway behind the main street, was built in Norman times. The church's dedication to St Giles possibly relates to the beechwoods which at one time covered the surrounding hillsides, St Giles being the patron saint of woodlands, as well as of the sick, poor and cripples. In the churchyard is the resting place of Bertram Mills who staged circuses at Olympia every year from 1920 until the 1980s.
Milton's Cottage – John Milton fled the Great Plague of London in 1665 and rented this 16th-century timber cottage. Here he completed *Paradise Lost*, his greatest work and started *Paradise Regained*. The cottage was bought by public subscription in 1877 to save it from being dismantled and taken to America. It is now administered by a trust and contains a number of relics and personal possessions, including a lock of the poet's hair, first editions of both poems, portraits and busts. The cottage is open to the public from Wednesday to Sunday, March to October.

REFRESHMENTS:
There are plenty of opportunities in Chalfont St Giles.

Walk 10   HUGHENDEN   3m (5km)

Maps: OS Sheets Landranger 165; Explorer 3.

The ridges of the Hughenden valley to Downley Common.

Start: At 865955, Hughenden Church.

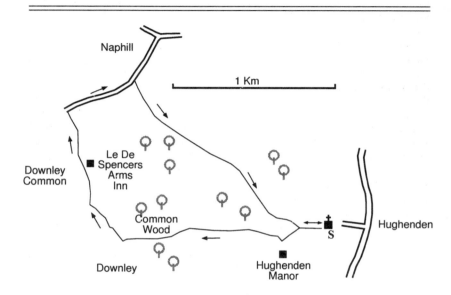

Park at the car park of the **Church of St Michael and All Angels, Hughenden**, and take the path into the churchyard, keeping the church on your right. Go through a metal gate into a field and continue through a wooden gate. Bear left along a tarmac drive, passing the Old Vicarage and **Hughenden Manor** on your left. Continue ahead between the brick and flint walls to join a path going steeply downhill. Keep to the main sunken path, ignoring all turnings and continuing ahead at a crossing path. On leaving the wood, take the fenced path along the valley bottom to enter Common Wood. Take a right fork along a level path into the centre of the wood and, at the next crossing path, turn right, uphill. Bear left at the next fork, then, nearing the top, bear left to go through a grassy area. Now walk ahead, through a gap in the hedge, to emerge on Downley Common. On reaching a gravel track, continue ahead passing in front of a row of cottages to join a tarmac road. Follow this past the Le De Spencers

Arms Inn and a row of houses, then take the path beneath the trees, following the white waymarker arrows. Go between five wooden posts and, after 60 yards, at a clear area, take the broad path ahead, as indicated by the white arrow.

Go past old saw pits on either side and then through wooden posts to emerge at a turning circle. Turn right down the tarmac lane and, after 500 yards, ignore a path to the right at the bottom of the hill, to turn right along a fenced path just after the house 'Braeside'. Cross a stile and follow the right edge of the field beyond. The path soon follows the edge of Flagmore Wood, part of the Hughenden Estate. Ignore a stile to the right entering the wood, but cross the stile in the corner, maintaining direction along the side of the wood. Do not cross the next stile on the right: instead, bear diagonally left across the field, going uphill and heading for a large oak tree. Go over the stile 30 yards to the right of the tree, cross a farm track and go through a kissing gate. Bearing right into the corner of the field beyond, go through a kissing gate and follow a downhill path into Hanging Wood. At a crossing path, continue ahead, ignoring a stile into the field on the left. Go through a gate, cross a tarmac road and bear left along a path through the churchyard to return to the start.

POINTS OF INTEREST:

Church of St Michael and All Angels, Hughenden – The church is of medieval origin, but only parts of the 14th-century North Chapel and 16th-century arcading are original. The most noteworthy of the memorials, in the chancel, is to Benjamin Disraeli. This white marble memorial was donated by Queen Victoria and is unique in being the only example of a memorial erected to a subject by a reigning monarch. The inscription reads '...his grateful and affectionate sovereign and friend Victoria RI' Beside the memorial hangs a banner and the insignia of the Order of the Garter, removed from Windsor Castle at the express wish of Queen Victoria. Outside the church is the Disraeli family vault and the tomb of Benjamin.

Hughenden Manor – This was the site of a plain British farmhouse until 1738 when the farming estate was converted to a gentleman's park. Benjamin Disraeli purchased the estate in 1848 with the help of a £25,000 loan from the Bentinck family. In 1862, the plain house was dramatically converted, by EB Lamb, into what Disraeli considered to be a Jacobean style residence. He entertained Queen Victoria in the house in 1877. Of the 18th-century interior, only a fireplace and plaster ceiling in the library remain. The house passed to the National Trust in 1946.

REFRESHMENTS:
Le De Spencers Arms Inn, Downley Common.
There is a tea room at Hughenden Manor when the house is open.

Walk 11   **STAPLEFORD**   3m (5km)

Maps OS Sheets: Landranger 166; Pathfinder 1096.
A charming short walk along the banks of the River Beane.
Start: At 313168, St Mary the Virgin Church, Stapleford.

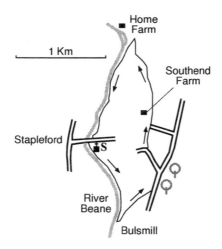

Follow the path to the right of the church, heading down to the River Beane. Keep to the main path (part of a **Nature Trail**), following the line of the river and ignoring all turnings. After leaving a wooded area, bear left to go slightly uphill. Go through a gap by a metal gate and turn left along a well-worn concrete track. Where the track goes left, continue ahead, crossing the corner of a field along a well-defined path to reach a lane. Turn left, soon forking left along a road signed for **Stapleford**.

Where the lane turns sharp left, ignore a path to the right and continue ahead along a gravel track towards Southend Farm. Go over a crossing path, passing the farm on your left, continuing along the gravel track. Ignore more paths on the left, continuing ahead along the drive to Home Farm. Turn left over a stile beneath the trees, just before the river.

Turn left and go through a kissing gate, continuing with the river on your right. The river is much wider here and contains a good stock of coarse fish, roach, rudd, bream and carp. The fishing is syndicated among just 50 anglers.

On reaching a wall, use the high steps and continue along a fenced path, passing a weir on your right. Ignore a crossing path and footbridge, continuing along a path which follows the line of the river. Leave an open area to enter Clusterbolt Wood, going along a delightful path with the river still on your right. On reaching a small housing estate, continue basically ahead, still following the line of the river, to reach a road by the church.

POINTS OF INTEREST:

Nature Trail – Leaflets describing the Trail and detailing the various marker points, are to be found by the notice board in front of the church. The Trail runs southwards from the church, following the River Beane.

Stapleford – This is one of the county's newer villages, consisting mainly of houses constructed after the 1914-18 War for returning soldiers. The village is centred around St Mary's Church, whose annual flower festival, held in May, attracts many visitors. Today many villagers work for the nearby Woodhall Estate.

REFRESHMENTS:

None directly on the route, but *The Woodhall Arms,* on the A119, can be found in the northern section of Stapleford village.

29

Walk 12   **WEST WYCOMBE**   3$^1/_2$m (5km)
Maps: OS Sheets Landranger 165 and 175; Explorer 3.
A scenic walk with two climbs.
Start: At 826947, the public car park next to the West Wycombe
Garden Centre, off the A40.

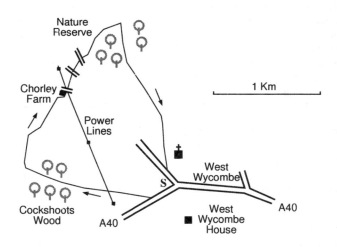

The start lies along the A40 from High Wycombe towards Oxford. Go through West
Wycombe village and turn right, bearing left at the foot of the grassy slopes of
Wycombe Hill. The car park is on your left. From it, turn right down to the A40. Turn
right, with care, passing the old pound used for enclosing stray animals. After 150 yards,
take the signed footpath over the stile on the right, diagonally crossing a field. Go
through a gap in the hedge and maintain direction across the next field, joining a
hedge on the left. Follow this path to the edge of Cockshoots Wood. Pause for breath
and look back: West Wycombe Church is to the left, the town of High Wycombe is
ahead and West Wycombe House and Park are to the right.

   Turn right, following the edge of the wood. Do not go through the first gap:
instead, continue for a further 50 yards to reach a stile. Cross into the wood and

follow the waymarked path, ignoring all turnings to arrive at a sunken bridleway. Turn right and, after a few paces, where the track forks, maintain direction by way of the right-hand fork. Follow this main track (note the animal tracks on either side) to the top of the hill and then downhill, passing Chorley Farm on your left to reach a lane.

Cross the lane into a paddock, following its left edge and keeping to the left of a power line pylon. Leave the field over the stile on to a lane. Cross this and a stile into the next field, crossing it to reach another stile. Cross a third lane and a stile, then follow the hedge on your right, going uphill to reach a gate into Butler's Hangings Nature Reserve. Continue uphill, bearing left through an area of natural chalk grassland. Go through the gate into the wood and continue to reach a crossing track. Turn right along a wide, waymarked path, going through a new plantation. In wet weather there is a parallel path to the right. After rounding several bends, **West Wycombe Church** can be seen through the trees directly ahead.

On reaching a way marker post, you have two choices of descent. To visit the church, continue ahead to reach a grass car park at the top of West Wycombe Hill, in front of the church with the **Mausoleum** behind it, to the left. To return to the start, walk down the hill on one of the grassy paths, then turn right across the bottom of the hill. Now cross the road: the car park is in front of you. Alternatively, bear right at the marker post, then left through a horse barrier, going downhill through an avenue of overhanging trees and bushes. When you emerge on the grassy slopes of the hill, turn right on one of the paths and cross the road to reach the starting car park.

POINTS OF INTEREST:

West Wycombe Church – The Church of St Lawrence was extensively restored by Sir Francis Dashwood, the second Baronet, in 1761. Its interior was inspired by the Temple of the Sun at Palmyra near Damascus, built in the 3rd century AD. The chancel and lower part of the tower date from 1350 and were incorporated into the new building. The golden ball crowning the tower is 8ft in diameter and is similar to the Ball of Fortune on a tower by the Grand Canal in Venice.

The Mausoleum – Completed in 1765 the Mausoleum was built using a £500 legacy from George Duddington, a member of the infamous 'Hell Fire Club'. The heart of another member, the poet Paul Whitehead, was set into the walls.

REFRESHMENTS:

There are several possibilities in West Wycombe High Street and a tea shop at the Garden Centre.

Walk 13   **FORTY GREEN** $3^1/_2$m (5km)

Maps: OS Sheets Landranger 175; Explorer 3.

A short walk passing, probably the country's oldest inn.

Start: At 917933, opposite Penn Holy Trinity Church.

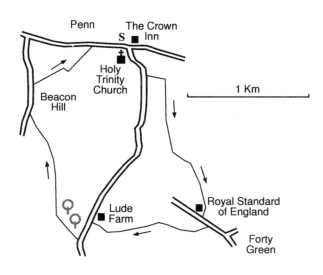

The church lies on the road between Penn and Knotty Green. Parking is available on the road beside the church or, with the landlord's permission, in the Crown Inn car park. Facing **Penn Holy Trinity Church**, go down the road between the church and the war memorial. Soon after passing 'The Knoll' and an S-bend, turn left along the path to the left of the vicarage. Follow the path to a T-junction and turn right along a tarmac track. Where this track bears left to a private drive, ignore a path to the right and continue ahead, keeping the barns on your right. The path follows the edge of the wood and soon bears right across the woodland corner. At a fork, bear right and cross a stile into a field. Bear left and head for an oak tree at the boundary corner and then go downhill to reach a stile in the field corner. Cross and follow a narrow path between houses, soon turning right to reach a lane. You now pass one of the country's oldest inns, **The Royal Standard of England**.

Turn left along the lane for 150 yards, then turn right and cross a stile into a small orchard. Bear right, downhill, keeping to the right of an electric cable post, then cross a stile and follow the line of the cables. Ignore two paths on the right and cross a metal stile into a field. Cross a stile in the valley bottom, then walk uphill with a hedge on your right. In the top corner, cross a stile and head towards Lude Farm. Where the track bears right, go over a stile on the left and cross the small paddock beyond to reach a stile by a metal gate.

Cross and turn left along a lane. After 150 yards, just before a left bend, turn right along a signed footpath. Follow the fence on your right to reach a stand of trees, and immediately beyond them go over a stile. Cross the centre of the field beyond, then another stile to reach a fenced path by a vineyard. The path soon joins a farm track. Follow this, ignoring a footpath on the right, but where the track bears left, continue ahead before bearing left across a field to reach a stile. Cross and walk through an area of scrub to reach a stile on to a road with modern houses.

Turn right towards the village of Penn, then, immediately after a telephone box, turn right to a gravel parking area. Bear right, and immediately left by a laurel hedge to join a footpath. Go over a stile, then keep left of a large oak to cross another stile. Turn right and, at the next fork, bear left, going uphill to meet a road. Turn right soon returning to Holy Trinity Church.

POINTS OF INTEREST:

Holy Trinity Church – Penn House and the right to appoint the vicar of Holy Trinity Church were a gift to Sybil Penn (Elizabeth I's governess) from Henry VIII. Much of the church dates back to the 11th century, though the tower is 15th-century. From it the locals say the views extends over 12 counties. Inside the church is a rare example of a plain leaden font and some old brasses commemorating the Penn family.

The Royal Standard of England – In 1875 the village consisted of only 10 houses and the public house. It is believed that the Ship Inn, dating back to 1213, stood on the site. The present name originates from the Civil War: the inn was the headquarters of the Royalists and was named the Standard by the soldiers. Legend has it that King Charles hid in the roof during his escape to France after the Battle of Worcester in 1651. After the restoration of the monarchy the name Royal – unique to the public house – was bestowed on the inn by the new King in gratitude.

REFRESHMENTS:
The Crown, Penn.
The Royal Standard of England, Forty Green.

Walk 14   **WINCHMORE HILL** $3\frac{1}{2}$m (5km)

Maps: OS Sheets Landranger 165 and 175; Explorer 3.

An ideal evening walk through woodland, ending at two inns.

Start: At 933949, opposite the Plough Inn and the Potters Arms.

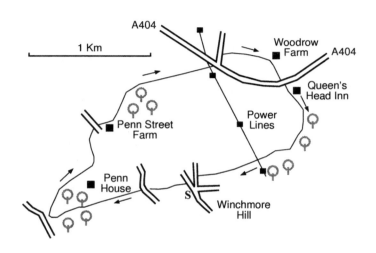

Parking is possible on the side of the common opposite the two inns. Cross the common opposite the Plough Inn to reach a footpath to the left of a wooden seat. Cross a stile and the centre of the field beyond, then cross another stile on to a road. Cross the road and a stile by a metal gate, then bear right over a stile into a large field. Bear slightly left to head for Pennhouse Grove. Go over a stile, cross the tarmac drive to Penn House and go over another stile. Cross a field corner to reach a stile into a wood. Follow a path downhill, walking with a fence on the right, then, before reaching a road, turn sharp right, uphill, along a marked bridleway. Ignore all joining paths, maintaining direction with views of **Penn House** through the trees on the right.

On leaving the wood, go through an avenue of tall trees to reach Garden Cottage. There, bear left staying on the track to reach a road by Penn Street Farm. Cross this busy road, with care, and follow a footpath to the left of a pair of brick and flint cottages, keeping left of the new cow barns – beware of the electric fences. Head for the corner of the trees to go over a stile. Ignore a kissing gate on the right, continuing

34

ahead with a wood on your right. Go over a stile and continue uphill, soon leaving the wood edge and heading for a line of electric pylons. Go under the main cables and bear left along a gravel track, to reach a road (the A404).

Cross this busy road, with great care, and go along the lane (Woodrow) opposite. After 30 yards, before Woodrow Farm Cottage, turn right over a stile and bear right to cross a stile in the corner. Walk with a fence on your right and, after 25 yards, cross a stile into a field. Bear diagonally right to reach a stile in a wire fence and follow the fence down to reach the A404 again. Cross (again with care) to the footpath sign opposite the Queen's Head. Take the path towards the inn, through an area of scrub, then keep to the right of both the inn and four terraced cottages to join a path to the left of four garages. Cross a stile and turn left before a second stile to follow a path uphill into a wood. Bear right at a fork, continuing uphill, then go over a stile, staying on the well-defined path. Just after the path bends left, turn right along a crossing track. Leave the wood, keeping right of the hedge in front to join a field edge path. Go through a gap in the hedge and continue, with the village of Winchmore Hill ahead. The path narrows to go between a factory and gardens, before reaching a road. Turn left opposite the chapel to reach, after 50 yards, the Plough Inn.

POINTS OF INTEREST:

Penn House – This was given to Sybil Penn, governess to Queen Elizabeth I, as a wedding present by Henry VIII. The most famous member of the family was William Penn who was persecuted for preaching Quakerism and sought escape by securing from Charles II the grant and charter of Pennsylvania. It was intended that Pennsylvania, together with Philadelphia, should be a holy experiment based on Quaker principles. Things did not go well and Penn found himself in an English jail. He died in 1712 and is buried at the Quaker's church at nearby Jordans.

REFRESHMENTS:

The Plough Inn, Winchmore Hill.
The Potters Arms, Winchmore Hill.
The Queen's Head, on the A404.

Walk 15   **BRILL** $3^1/_2$m (5km)

Maps: OS Sheets Landranger 165; Pathfinder 1093.

Starting some 600 feet above sea level, the walk descends into the valley west of Brill, then climbs back to the windmill.

Start: At 652142, Brill Windmill.

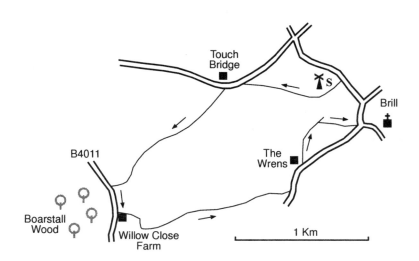

Walk behind the **windmill** to reach a wood-clad house. Turn left and pass a small cottage, then turn right along a track. After passing the vine-covered garden wall of another cottage, turn right to cross a stile, following the 'circular walk' waymarkers. Keep to the right of an intermittent line of trees, then bear left and cross a stile into a larger field. Go diagonally right to cross a stile in a wooden fence and follow a prominent path downhill. Go over a footbridge and bear left, to cross a stile into a small grouping of trees. On reaching a road, turn left and, where the road bends sharply to the right after 100 yards, go ahead along to a track named Span Green. This track is reasonably wide, but can get very muddy after rain. Where the main track bears left to go into a field, continue ahead along a narrow path between hedges. Now as you reach a more open area, follow the main, occasionally waymarked, path, ignoring any turnings, to reach a road (the B4011). Turn left, with care, for 300 yards, then turn left over a stile beside Willow Close Farm. Cross the drive to the farm and go over a stile, a footbridge and another stile into a field.

Go over a ladder stile, across a grass track and over the stile ahead and aim for the solitary dead tree. Cross a footbridge and walk uphill with a hedge on your left. At the top, go over a stile and continue uphill through the next field. At the waymarker post, bear right along a farm track. There are splendid views from here, stretching from Buckinghamshire and the Chiltern Hills to Oxfordshire and the Cotswolds. At the end of the track, go over a cattle grid to reach a road. Turn left and, soon after passing a large house (The Wrens), cross a stile on the left and bearing left to cross another stile on to a narrow uphill path. Go over a stile and continue through a small copse. Cross a stile and continue along a gravel track, turning right after 20 yards to follow a downhill path. The path, along the rear gardens of houses, emerges by a row of terraced bungalows: continue ahead along a gravel, then fenced, path to reach a road. Turn left towards the centre of **Brill**. Turn left at the War Memorial and, after 150 yards, turn left again along Windmill Street to return to the start.

POINTS OF INTEREST:

Brill Windmill – The site, 600 feet above sea level, is ideal for a windmill. The present mill was built in 1680, the body being fixed to a vertical post enabling the sails to be turned around to face the wind. The first round house base was added in 1865: the present one was built in 1948. The mill was used for milling barley until 1919. The pits and undulations on the common around the mill are a result of the clay extraction for the local brick and tile industry. The local pottery industry dates back to the 13th century and remains of brick kilns of the 13th- and 14th-centuries have been found. Many of the older houses in the village were constructed of Brill bricks, as was nearby Waddesdon Manor. Many years ago the common around the mill was also quarried, the deep undulations still being visible today. Villagers retain grazing rights on the common and refuse to have the grass levelled as this would reduce the area of grass available.

Brill – All Saints' Church is Norman in origin, having been built in the 12th century. The tower was added in the 15th century, while the roof is 17th-century. The church was restored in 1889 by J O Scott.

REFRESHMENTS:

The Pheasant Inn, by the Windmill car park at the start.
There are also several possibilities in Brill.

Walk 16   MAIDENHEAD   3¹/₂m (5km)

Maps: OS Sheets Landranger 175; Explorer 3.

An easy walk along field paths and tracks, with the final stretch along the Thames towpath.

Start: At 902813, in River End by Maidenhead Bridge.

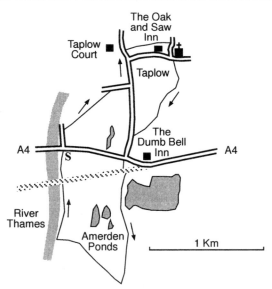

Parking is possible in River End. Return to the bridge and cross the main road (the A4), with great care, into Mill Lane, following it past the sadly derelict Skindles Hotel. On the bend, by the entrance to Mill Lane Boat Yard, turn right through a kissing gate and go along a fenced path with the gas works on your left. Go through a swing gate and follow the well-defined path beyond across the centre of a field. After a short climb, go through a kissing gate and turn right along the lane to reach a T-junction. Turn left, uphill, passing Rectory Road on the right. After a further 40 yards, turn right along a footpath. (**Taplow Court** is another 30 yards up the road.)

    Follow the path, walking with a wall, and, soon, a wooden fence, on your right, passing some playing fields on the left. At a fork, continue ahead with a school and the spire of **Taplow Church** on the right. On reaching a lane, turn right to pass the church. Follow the lane to a T-junction. The Oak and Saw Inn is on the right here. Cross the road and take the path between the telephone box and St Nicholas House. Go through a kissing gate and immediately turn right across the corner of a field, going through another kissing gate and following a path between intermittent hedges. Go through a kissing gate and bear right along a well-used path. Go through yet another kissing gate to reach a road. Turn left to reach the A4. To the left are two inns, the Dumb Bell and the Old Station Inn.

Cross the road, with great care, and follow the track opposite under the railway. Continue with a lake on your left, following the track for nearly a mile to reach a fork. Turn right and, after a few yards, turn sharp right along a wide path across the centre of a field. Go through a gap and continue with a wire fence on your left. Cross a footbridge and, at the next field corner, bear left through a gap. Follow a path with a wire fence on your right, continuing between houses and stables to reach the Thames towpath. Turn right along this gravel path, with the Thames and some splendid riverside houses on your left. Go under the **Brunel Railway Bridge** and continue into River End and the start.

POINTS OF INTEREST:

Taplow Court – The Court is built on the site of the original manor house. The estate, including what is today the Cliveden Estate, was very extensive. In the grounds is Bapsey Pond where, the story has it, in Roman times, St Birinius baptised his followers.

Taplow Church – The church, dedicated to St Nicholas, was originally sited on the estate, but in 1828 it was demolished and rebuilt on the present site in the centre of the village.

Brunel Railway Bridge – The bridge was designed by IK Brunel in 1838. Only two spans were included in the design in order to avoid unnecessary interference with navigation. The brick arches are the widest and flattest in the world, each span being 128 feet, with a rise of only 24 feet.

REFRESHMENTS;

The Oak and Saw Inn, Taplow.
The Dumb Bell Inn, on the A4.
The Old Station Inn, on the A4.
There is also a wide variety of possibilities in Maidenhead.

Walk 17   STOKE POGES $3^{1}/_{2}$m (5km)

Maps: OS Sheets Landranger 175; Explorer 3.

An easy walk along field paths passing some historic properties.

Start: At 978827, Stoke Poges Church and Gardens car park.

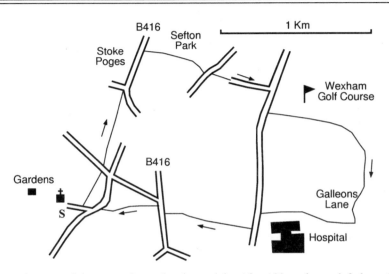

From the car park, return to the road and turn right. After 100 yards turn left through a kissing gate. The **Monument** is on the left as you cross the field. Follow the path to the right of the oak tree and continue across the middle of the field. Go through a kissing gate in the corner to reach the B416. Cross the road, with care, to the gate opposite. Go through and follow the left edge of the field beyond, passing the Clock House on the left. Go through a gate, and then through a gap in the corner. Cross a footbridge to reach a kissing gate. Go through and maintain direction to go through another gate. Bear right to reach a gate in the corner. Go through and cross Rogers Lane, continuing ahead up the main road (the B416). Just beyond the bus shelter, cross the road, with care, and turn right along a path, crossing a recreation area within **Sefton Park**. Bear right at a fork and go through a pair of gates. In the corner, turn right along to a sunken track. Cross a stile and Farthing Green Lane, and go along the bridle way opposite. Continue ahead along a road to reach a T-junction with the Plough Inn on the left.

Turn right and, at the end of the houses, turn left along a signed footpath. Cross a stile and the golf course car park, keeping the clubhouse on your left. Go past the driving range and, in the corner of the car park, follow the track across the centre of the course. Where the track turns right, continue ahead across a fairway to reach a stile in the hedge by a single silver birch tree. Cross and turn right along a bridleway (Galleons Lane). After passing the buildings of Bell Farm, turn right over a stile and follow a wide path soon joining a concrete drive, passing Wexham Hospital, on the left, to reach a road. Turn left and, after 100 yards, turn right over a stile. Go over a stile by an oak tree (the going can be very muddy here) and continue along the left edge of a field. Cross a stile and the corner of the field beyond to reach a stile by a wooden gate. At the junction of paths beyond, continue ahead down the tarmac drive to reach a road (the B416 again). Turn right and, after 30 yards, cross, with care, and turn left along to a stony track signed for Duffield Park. Follow the track through two swing gates to return to the starting car park at the **Church** and **Gardens**.

POINTS OF INTEREST:

Monument – The monument in the National Trust field was erected in 1799 by John Penn, a grandson of the founder of Pennsylvania William Penn, to honour Thomas Grey. It was restored in 1977 following an appeal launched by Sir John Betjeman.

Sefton Park – Originally known as Stoke Farm, the house was built for Lady Molyneux, daughter of the Earl of Sefton. The well-known actress Vesta Tilley once lived in the house. During the 1939-45 War the Gordon Highlanders and American GIs were stationed here prior to the invasion of Normandy, visits being made to the house by several famous war leaders.

St Giles Church – The church is famous for its connection with Thomas Grey the poet who died in 1771 and who lies buried under a stone slab with his mother and aunt. The tomb is outside the east end of the church. His famous *Elegy written in a Country Churchyard* with the opening lines' The curfew tolls the knell of parting day' is one of the best-known poems in the English Language.

Stoke Poges Memorial Gardens – Situated next to the church, the gardens were founded by Sir Noel Mobbs to preserve for all time the peace and serenity of the ancient church of St Giles. There is a small charge to visit.

REFRESHMENTS:
The Plough Inn, Wexham Street.

Walk 18   **CHENIES**   3$^1/_2$m (5km)

Maps: OS Sheets Landranger 166; Pathfinder 1139.

Wood and field paths to the east of Chenies, following, in part, the River Chess.

Start: At 016984, the Village Green, Chenies.

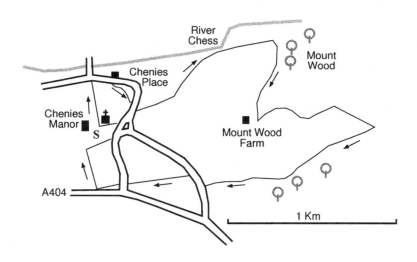

With your back to the village pump, turn left, cross the road and follow a gravel track, keeping the village school on your left. Go past **St Michael's Church**, on the right, then, with **Chenies Manor House** in front of you, turn right along a walled pathway. Follow the path downhill and, at the three-way fork, continue ahead. Go over a crossing path, continuing downhill to reach a road. Turn right, walking with the River Chess on your left.

Bear right with the road to go uphill and, after 100 yards, opposite Chenies Place, bear right up some steps and go along a signed footpath. Follow this path through a wood to reach a road. Cross and turn sharp left, up a single track tarmac lane (Holloway Lane). Ignore a crossing path, continuing along the lane, which follows a woodland edge. At the end of the wood, turn right over a stile, going downhill, to

42

reach a stile in the hedge opposite. Cross and turn right, rejoining, Holloway Lane. Continue along the lane, with the River Chess on your left. Where the track bears left, at the edge of Mount Wood, bear right through a gap. Do not cross the stile: instead, turn right along an uphill path, walking with a wire fence on your left. Keep to the main path (which is waymarked with white arrows) through the wood. Cross a stile to leave the wood and head for the left corner of Mount Wood Farm. Cross a stile and turn left along a stony track.

At the edge of a small wood, cross a stile between metal gates and follow the path beyond, keeping the wood on your right. Go through a gap and bear left, away from the wood, keeping a hedge on your left. After 250 yards the path bears right away from the hedge into the bottom right-hand corner of the field: cross a stile and immediately turn right into the wood, which is known as Nicholas Spring. Leave the wood and bear left to reach a marker post. Bear right, heading uphill to the corner of a wood. Cross a stile to go along the right edge of Wyburn Wood. Cross a stile and continue along the right edge of a field. Go over a stile and through a swing gate to reach a road. Turn right. (The Red Lion Inn can be seen ahead.) Turn left along the side of the playing fields and go through a kissing gate. Now maintain direction, crossing a stile to the left of the right-hand corner of the field. Go along a narrow path to reach a road. Cross and continue ahead to reach the main road (the A404). Turn right and, after 10 yards, turn right up a gravel track. Turn right at the bridleway marker, with Chenies Manor on your left. Follow the bridleway to a road and turn left. The Village Green is now in front of you.

POINTS OF INTEREST:

St Michael's Church, Chenies – It is believed that a wooden Saxon church stood on this site. The present church was built in 1556. Although the Duke of Bedford sold his Chenies estate in 1954, it is in the Bedford Chapel, within the church, that the Dukes are laid to rest among their ancestors. The Chapel contains some fine memorials to the Russell family.

Chenies Manor House – The House is Tudor in origin, L-shaped and built of red brick with steep gables and ornamental brick chimneys. For many years the House was the seat of the Russell family, the Earls and Dukes of Bedford. The House contains many portraits of the family, together with numerous personal pieces. The house is open on Wednesday and Thursday afternoons and also on Bank Holiday Mondays.

REFRESHMENTS:
The Red Lion, Chenies.
The Bedford Arms, Chenies.

Walk 19   **St Paul's Walden** $3\frac{1}{2}$m (5km)

Maps: Os Sheets Landranger 166; Pathfinder 1072.

South from St Paul's Walden, to stroll along the charming main street at Whitwell. Returning past the imposing Stagenhoe House.

Start: At 193223, All Saints' Church, St Paul's Walden.

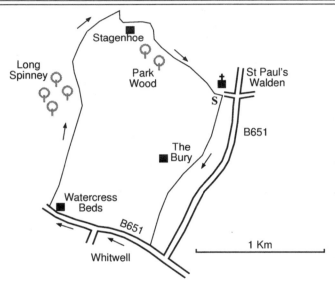

There is a large car park close to the church. Take the wide track opposite the church, going slightly downhill. The statues of Venus and Adonis in the woodland garden of **The Bury** can be seen on the right. Follow the track around to the right of the green triangle, then go uphill, joining a tarmac and gravel track. (There are better views of The Bury from the top of the hill.) Ignore a kissing gate on the left, continuing along the track, then, where it bends right to a house, continue ahead through a kissing gate. Keep to the left edge of the field beyond and go through a kissing gate in the corner. Continue downhill along a temporary fenced path, heading towards the village of Whitwell. Go over a stile and a crossing track, and cross a small paddock. Go over a stile and cross the River Mimram. Bear left and cross a paddock to reach a stile by a metal gate. Cross and bear right along a gravel track, passing between houses to reach a road (the B651).

Turn right along the road (Whitwell High Street), ignoring a footpath on the left. Continue along the High Street, passing the Bull Inn, the Maidens Head Inn, the Post Office and stores and the Eagle and Child Inn. After passing the **Whitwell watercress beds**, turn right, just after the brick cottage, along a path signed for Preston. Follow this wide track for something over a mile, passing Long Spinney, on the left, and **Stagenhoe**, to the right. The track goes downhill after the spinney and then bears right, uphill, towards Park Wood, on the left. Cross the track leading to Stagenhoe and follow a well-worn, sunken path along the edge of the wood. At the end of the field on the left, by a marker post, turn right through a gap. Keep to the left of a clump of trees and turn left at another marker post to follow the perimeter fence of the house. Continue down the drive to reach the tennis courts. Here, turn right down a gravel track, keeping Garden Wood on your right. The track joins a lane by a recently converted house: continue ahead to reach the **church**.

POINTS OF INTEREST:
The Bury, St Pauls Walden – The earliest part of the house now remaining is the north wing, built in 1767. The main section of this imposing, Adam-style house was built in 1887. It is the home of the Bowes Lyon family, the Queen Mother spending part of her childhood here.
Whitwell Watercress Beds – The beds, which are still in production, were first used in the 18th century. The watercress was sold in the streets of London at the turn of the century for a halfpenny a bunch.
Stagenhoe – Now a Sue Ryder Home for the physically handicapped, the house was formerly the seat of the Earl of Caithness. It burnt down in 1737 and was rebuilt in 1740. At one time it was the home of Sir Arthur Sullivan, the composer. It is said that he composed the music for the *Mikado* here.
All Saints' Church, St Paul's Walden – The church dates back to the 12th century, but has greatly changed by alteration and restoration. A wall tablet dated 1900 commemorates the baptism of the Queen Mother in the 15th-century font.

REFRESHMENTS:
The Strathmore Arms, St Pauls Walden.
The Bull Inn, Whitwell.
The Maidens Head, Whitwell.
The Eagle and Child, Whitwell.

Walk 20   **ASHENDON** $3^1/_2$m ($5^1/_2$km)

Maps: OS Sheets Landranger 165; Explorer 2.

Around the hill top village of Ashendon, with views of Waddesdon Manor.

Start: At 705144, the Gatehangers Inn.

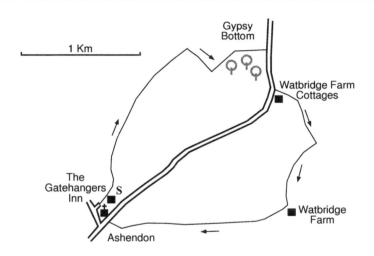

If you are using the inn's large car park, please check with the landlord beforehand. Walk between the **Gatehangers Inn** and Cherry Cottage, passing the Post Office on the left. Now take the footpath, to the right of Temple Cottage and cross a stile into a sloping paddock. Bear left to cross a stile to the left of a large bush in the hedge then turn left to go through a metal gate. After 40 yards, bear right to cross a stile, a footbridge and another stile. Now bear left, keeping to the right of the farm buildings, to cross a stile between the two trees in a field boundary. Bear left across the field beyond and go through a gap in the hedge, heading towards a wire-fenced compound. Follow the fence around to the right and, where the fence bears left, cross a stile over a section of post and rail fencing. Turn right and, in the corner of the field, cross a stile into Gypsy Bottom.

Follow a path beside a high wire fence, continuing ahead where the fence turns left to reach a footbridge. Cross the bridge on to a road. Turn right along the road and, after 250 yards, just before the road bends right, turn left down a concrete track signed for Watbridge Farm, passing Watbridge Cottages on the right. Remain on this track, ignoring all turnings off, until you reach some farm buildings. Bear left here, going over a cattle grid and then bearing right to continue along the concrete track, to reach Watbridge Farm.

Keeping the farm on the left, turn right at a cattle grid to go along a field edge and then follow the path through a metal gate to reach a stile in the hedge. Cross this, a footbridge and another stile, then bear left across the corner of a field to reach a wooden gate. Go through the gate and cross a footbridge into a field. Now, generally heading for Ashendon, seen on the hill ahead, bear right to cross a footbridge and go over a stile into a field. Bear left to reach a metal gate on a line between two large oak trees and continue to reach a stile to the side of the right-hand oak tree. Keep left of the brow of the hill and follow a path uphill to a marker post. From the post, look back for an excellent view – Waddesdon is on the far left, with the valley ahead. Now head for **St Mary's Church**, crossing a stile and going along a narrow path to reach a road. Take the path to the right of the church and turn left before the village post office to return to the start.

POINTS OF INTEREST:

Gatehangers Inn – The inn was originally known as the Red Lion, changing its name very recently. It is perhaps no coincidence to learn of a recent village tradition to celebrate the belated hanging of a new gate to the allotments. After the gate was fixed by two villagers, having lain in the hedge for some years, it was decided that a dinner should be held annually to commemorate the event. Each year since 1962 the men of the village have therefore met for the Ashendon Gatehangers' dinner. Many charities and village activities have been helped and supported by the Gatehangers.

St Mary's Church – The church is of Saxon origin and is built of grey stone with a stumpy little tower. The interior has been heavily restored. The item of most interest, is the late 17th-century pulpit which remains in its original condition.

REFRESHMENTS:

The Gatehangers Inn, Ashendon.

Walk 21   **WENDOVER** $3^1/_2$m ($5^1/_2$km)

Maps: OS Sheets Landranger 165; Explorer 2.

A walk through Wendover Woods, following part of the Firecrest Trail.

Start: At 875082, Beechwood Lane, Wendover.

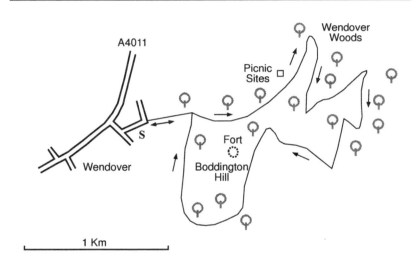

To reach the start, take slip road on the right after the Packhorse Inn, turn right into Collet Road and then left into Barlow Lane following it to its junction with Beechwood Lane. At the lane's right-angled bend, take the gravel bridle way on the right towards **Wendover Woods**. At the cottage at the end of the lane, take the left-hand path and follow it very steeply uphill. Cross a stile and continue ahead along an uphill path. Near the top, go over a crossing path (the Forest Fitness Trail), soon after turning left along a wide track. Go through a wooden barrier to reach a turning circle and continue ahead along a wide gravel track, passing two picnic sites on the left. At a junction, turn right, following a tarmac path round to the left. Ignore a track joining from the right and, after 20 yards, turn right at a Forestry Commission notice board headed **Firecrest Trail**. It is possible to miss this turning and notice board as it is slightly offset to the road, so please be careful.

The path is well-defined and marked with a mauve representation of the firecrest. Go downhill at first, then keep right at the fork by the second marker post, going along a level path through the conifers. Go over a crossing track, continuing ahead and still following the marker posts. Keep to the right of the badger viewing platform, soon going steeply downhill and crossing a track. Continue ahead, bearing left and still following the marker posts, with a clearing on your right. Bear left at another marker post, soon passing marker No. 4. Now, after a further 20 yards, turn right along a gravel track. Follow this track along the valley bottom, passing post No. 5 on the left. After a further 50 yards, bear right off the track, to go along a marked footpath. Turn right at a T-junction and, after 150 yards, turn left along a wide track. Go past marker post No. 7 and, after a further 50 yards, turn right along a narrow path going uphill through the heart of the conifer wood. Cross a track and continue ahead, passing marker post No. 8, with fields on your left. There are excellent views from this point of the walk.

Go past marker post No. 9 and a wooden seat and, on reaching the next crossing track, turn left, uphill, leaving the Firecrest Trail to reach a T-junction. Turn left along a level path and ignore a right fork to continue downhill along a signed bridleway. Bear left at a fork, still going downhill, and, on reaching a wood storage area, bear right away from a road to follow a track, keeping to the edge of the wood below Boddington Hill. At a crossing path, turn left over a stile to return to Beechwood Lane.

POINTS OF INTEREST:

Wendover Woods – The wood was originally owned by the Rothschild family, as part of the Halton Estate. It was transferred to the Forestry Commission in 1939. The wood contains a scheduled ancient monument known as Boddington Bank, an Iron Age hill fort. The wood offers stunning views over the Vale of Aylesbury and includes a number of waymarked walks, an orienteering course, a fitness trail, play areas and barbecue sites. Further information can be obtained from a copy of the Forestry Commission leaflet on the Chiltern Woodlands.

Firecrest Trail – Wendover Woods are now one of the most important nesting sites for the firecrest, one of our smallest birds. The firecrest nests in the tops of the Norway spruce. Woodland management plans have been amended to protect its nesting site and natural habitat. The Firecrest Trail focuses on the bird and other aspects of wildlife and conservation.

REFRESHMENTS:
There are numerous opportunities in Wendover.

Maps: OS Sheets Landranger 166; Pathfinder 1073.
A flat and easy walk, to the east of the 'old' village of Ardeley.
Startt: At 308272, St Lawrence's Church, Ardeley.

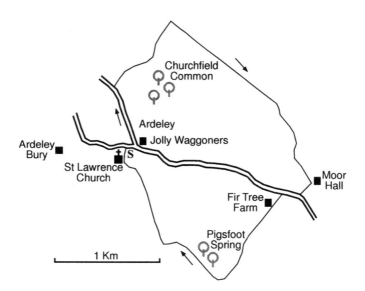

Parking is possible in the lay-by outside the church, between the Jolly Waggoners Inn and the thatched village hall. Return to the crossroads by the inn and turn left, before the inn, along the road signed for Cottered. Follow the road downhill for about 700 yards and, after crossing the Ardeley Brook, turn right along a track marked 'Private Track – No Bridleway'. Follow the track, with a brook on the right, to reach Churchfield Common (Woods) high on the right. Now, just after passing the first tree on the track, turn left along a well-marked path across a field. Ignore a track joining from the right and continue ahead, passing under the power cables. At a T-junction, turn right to pass beside a metal gate. Now follow the bridleway for about a mile, ignoring all turnings. Go over a bridge and pass a pair of benches, continuing ahead, slightly uphill. Ignore paths to both left and right, and, after 200 yards, turn right over a stile. Bear left to cross the field corner and go over a stile. Skirt a pond and cross a stile on the right, in the corner. Follow the footpath to reach a stile to the right of the wood corner opposite.

Cross on to a wide track and turn right to follow it between the farm buildings and Moor Hall, on the left, and the thatched farm house (Moorhall Cottage) on the right. Follow the track around to the right to reach a minor road. Turn right and, after 100 yards, turn left along a signed public by-way, passing Fir Tree Farm on the right. On entering a clearing, take the left-hand branch at a track fork. The track soon narrows to go through bushes. It can also be very rutted, being used by off-road vehicles. Continue past Pigsfoot Spring (a small wood) on the right to reach a crossing track. Turn right and, at the next track crossing, turn right again, keeping the hedge line on your right. The area behind the hedge here is often used as a driving course for quad bikes and go-karts.

Ardeley Church can now be seen on the skyline ahead: ignore a track joining from the left and continue ahead, going slightly uphill. Maintain direction at a three way fork, walking through a small cul-de-sac of houses and passing the village school at **Ardeley** to join the road. St Lawrence's Church is on your left.

POINTS OF INTEREST:

Ardeley – First time visitors to the village, are always impressed by the thatached cottages and village hall opposite the village pond. It would appear at first sight that they were built during the 19th century, but this is not so. They were, in fact, started in 1917 and completed in 1920. The houses were built on land given to the village by John Howard Carter, then owner of Ardeley Bury. Little remains of the original late Tudor brick house of Ardeley Bury. The later additions are the work of John Murray, the architect, in 1820.

The centre piece of the village green is the well house, a structure of brick and timber with a tiled roof. The well provided water for the residents of the Green for some years prior to the provision of piped water. The machinery used for raising the water is still in place.

St Lawrence's Church has a typical Hertfordshire tower with spike. The nave is 13th-century and some of the stained glass windows are 14th-century, Inside there are 16th-century brasses to Philip Metcalf, one of the church's vicars, and Thomas Shotbolt, together with his wife and children.

REFRESHMENTS:
The Jolly Waggoners Inn, Ardeley.

Maps: OS Sheets Landranger 165; Pathfinder 1093.

An easy walk to Ickford Bridge, with a return along the banks of the River Thame.

Start: At 667069, Shabbington Post Office.

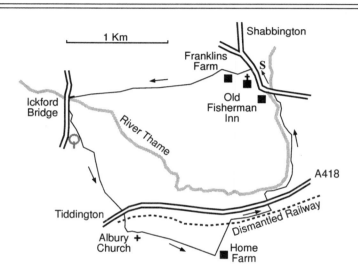

From the Post Office return to the main village road and turn left towards **St Mary Magdalene Church**. Go through the church gates and follow the path to the right to reach a stile into a field. Bear right towards Franklins Farm, crossing a footbridge and a stile. Cross a track and a ladder stile by a white metal gate, then go through two small paddocks and cross a stile by a horse jump. Bear left to cross a fence and a footbridge in the hedge, about 50 yards from the left field corner, then bear left to cross a track. Now maintain direction across a large field and cross a stile in the corner. Cross another two stiles and a footbridge, then turn left, following the line of a small stream. Cross a footbridge in the field corner and the centre of the field beyond, keeping to the left of a clump of trees. Turn right to follow the River Thame, then cross a concrete footbridge and a stile between the two arched bridges forming the ancient **Ickford Bridge** to reach a road.

Turn left, go over the bridge and walk along the road. Soon, turn left over a footbridge and a stile, then turn right along the edge of a wood. Cross a stile in the corner, by a metal gate, and bear left, keeping to the right of a new house, to join a concrete track. Follow this track through a metal gate and immediately turn left, through a gate, to go along a wide track between hedges. Go through a gate and, where the track bears left and ends, continue ahead through a metal gate, keeping a hedge on your left. In the field corner, cross a stile and, on reaching a lay-by, turn right to reach the main A418. Cross this busy road, with great care, and, after 50 yards, turn left, through a wooden gate and cross the field beyond to reach a gap in a hedge. Go over a dismantled railway and through a wooden gate, then continue ahead, passing a white cottage. Cross a stile and turn left along a tarmac track. Now ignore a sharp right turn and, where the gravel path goes left, bear left and then turn right along a path marked as part of the **Oxfordshire Way**. Cross a stile to the left of Albury Church and follow a fenced path uphill. Cross a stile and continue along a track for about $^1/_2$ mile, then, just before reaching Home Farm, turn left, on to a concrete track towards 'The Red House'. Go through a pair of metal gates and immediately turn right along a gravel path (the trackbed of the dismantled railway). Before reaching a wood, turn left down steps and follow a path to the A418. Cross, again with care, and follow the path opposite, marked as part of the Thame Valley Walk. Turn right in the corner, following the path along the bank of the River Thame to reach a road. Turn left, bearing right at the Old Fisherman Inn to return to the start in Shabbington.

POINTS OF INTEREST:
St Mary Magdalene Church – Restored and reseated in 1877, but some relics of the past remain – the old plaster and roof timbers in the nave, some of the stone work on the northern walls and the eastern part of the nave are probably Norman. There are also some early 14th-century windows and a pulpit dated 1626.

Ickford Bridge – A wooden bridge is known to have stood on this site as early as 1237. The present bridge is medieval, but was renovated in 1685. The bridge, which crosses the River Thame and the Oxfordshire border, is in two parts, the single arch Whirlpool Bridge and the multi-arch main bridge.

Oxfordshire Way – This 65-mile waymarked walk through rural Oxfordshire runs from Bourton-on-the-Water to Henley-on-Thames in the Chilterns. It was created in 1970 and is maintained by Oxfordshire County Council's Countryside Service.

REFRESHMENTS:
The Old Fisherman, by the River Thame at the end of the walk.

Walk 24   **BALLINGER COMMON**   4m (6km)

Maps: OS Sheets Landranger 165; Explorer 3.

A mixture of field and woodland paths along the valley at Pednor Bottom.

Start: At 913032, opposite the Pheasant Inn, Ballinger Common.

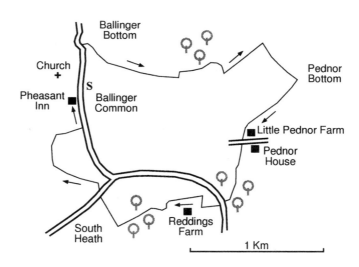

Parking is possible in the main street, or in Chiltern Road, a turning off the main street. Facing the Pheasant Inn, turn right along the road, walking downhill to Ballinger Bottom. At the S-bend, turn right along a farm track, with a stable block and cottage on your left. After 20 yards, turn right, uphill, along a winding track and, at a fork, bear right, uphill, into woodland. The path levels out beside some house rear gardens: cross a stile and walk along the right edge of the field beyond, then bear left to follow the hedge line into the field corner. Turn left, ignoring a stile to the right, and, after 30 yards, turn right over a stile into Bellows Wood. Now ignore a path on the left, continuing ahead along the wood edge. Ignore all turnings to reach a stile, crossing to exit the wood. Continue with a hedge and wire fence on your right, and, in the corner, ignore the track ahead and turn left, going downhill with a hedge on your right. At the foot of the hill, cross a stile and turn right along a wide bridleway. On joining a minor lane, continue ahead and, after 100 yards, at a crossing path, turn right over a stile. Go uphill with a hedge on your right, cross a stile in the corner and maintain direction along the right edge of the field beyond to cross a stile into a paddock. Go diagonally across the paddock, with Little Pednor Farm on your left. Go over a stile beneath an electricity pylon and follow a path along the left side of the field beyond to reach a road. Behind the hedge on the left are the remains of an ancient moat.

Turn left to view the impressive **Pednor House** and dovecote. Now retrace your steps to where you joined the road and go over a stile, now on the left. Follow a narrow path to reach a stile. Cross the stile and a new plantation, and go through a metal squeeze-type stile. Walk downhill to a similar stile. Beyond, cross a track and go through a gap in a fence into a wood. Follow the path beyond uphill through the wood to reach a road. Turn left, then, after 15 yards, turn right along a track towards Reddings Farm. Follow the re-routed path around a fenced paddock on the right and cross a stile. Turn right at a line of trees and, at the corner of a wood, cross a stile and bear left to follow a somewhat indistinct path occasionally waymarked with white arrows. At the edge of the wood, ignore a path on the left and bear right in front of a white cottage to reach a path at the rear of the houses. Cross a road and the stile opposite, bearing right across a small paddock to reach a stile in a fence. Bear left into a corner and cross a stile. Bear left to cross a double stile in a hedge, then bear right to head for the two oak trees. Cross a combined stile and turn right, now walking with a hedge on your left. Do not cross the stile on the left: instead, follow the hedge line into the field corner. Cross a stile on to a path between some very attractive properties, Ballinger House being on the left. At the road, turn left for a gentle stroll into **Ballinger Common**.

POINTS OF INTEREST:

Pednor House – Formally Little Pednor, the house is a 17th-century Tudor-framed and 18th-century brick property, but was substantially renovated and enlarged in 1911, notably along the south side of the large oblong courtyard. In the courtyard is a recently added dovecote.

Ballinger Common – The Common was at one time noted for its cherry orchards, the fruit being used for fine jams and renowned cherry pies. Only a few of the trees still remain and the pies are sadly no longer made.

REFRESHMENTS:

The Pheasant Inn, Ballinger Common.

OWLSWICK 4m (6km)

Maps: OS Sheets Landranger 165; Explorer 2.

A level walk along field paths, passing the site of the medieval village of Waldridge. The paths can be difficult to follow, so the Explorer map is recommended.

Start: At 789063, the Shoulder of Mutton Inn, Owlswick.

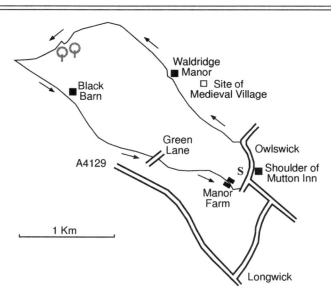

Owlswick is reached by turning off the A 4129 (Thame - Princes Risborough road) at Longwick. If you are using the inn car park please ask the permission of the landlord beforehand. Turn right along the road and, after 200 yards, at a right-hand bend, turn left along a gravel track. Where the track bears left (Swans Way), cross a stile on the right and follow a hedge. Where this bears right, continue ahead following a line of wooden posts. Near the far hedge, bear left to cross a stile beneath a clump of large trees. Cross the centre of the field beyond to reach a stile. Cross and continue ahead to cross another stile. Now bear right towards Waldridge Manor. The site of the **medieval village** of Waldridge is to the right of the Manor. Go through a metal gate to the left of the Manor and bear right, skirting a pond, to follow the line of the fence on the right.

Go under two sets of power lines and, in the corner, go over a post and rail fence and continue with a hedge on your right. In the next corner, go through a gap in the hedge and continue with the hedge on your left. Go through the gap in the corner and bear left to cross the centre of a field. To the left of the field corner, go through a gap in the wide hedge (this can be difficult to spot) and head across the field beyond to reach a small copse. Do not enter the copse: instead, turn right along its edge and go through a gate. The correct line of the footpath in this field is across the corner, but it is often very muddy and an alternative is to go along the left edge.

On reaching three large trees by the corner, turn left through a gap and go over a footbridge. Follow the left edge of the field and, where a hedge joins at a sharp angle from the left, turn left over a post and rail fence. Cross an electric fence and continue along the field's right edge, heading for an oak tree in front of tall poplars. Go through a gate by the oak, then through a gate by the ruins of Black Barn. Immediately turn right through a gate and go left to follow the left edge of a field. Cross a stile in the corner and continue ahead, passing under the electricity cables. Go through a gap in a hedge and on to the left corner of the field. Cross a stile, a small plantation, another stile and a footbridge. Now keep to the left of the large trees to cross a concrete track and a stile, following the line of a small drainage ditch. Cross the ditch, where it bends left, heading for a new plantation. Bear left to cross a stile, by a pair of oak trees and go through the plantation to reach a stile. Cross Green Lane, but do not go through the gate ahead: instead, turn right, and then left into the field, following its left edge. Cross a stile to reach an obvious stile in the hedge opposite. Cross and bear right across the corner of the field to go over a metal fence, heading towards Manor Farm. Cross a stile into a paddock, then go through a small wood and a wooden gate to join a lane. After 15 yards, turn left along a tarmac track, then turn left along the minor road into **Owlswick**. The Shoulder of Mutton Inn is on the right.

POINTS OF INTEREST:

Owlswick – The village name is of Scandinavian origin, from the personal name 'Ulf'. It is likely that Ulf owned property here.

Waldridge Medieval Village – The name has been spelt variously as Waldrudge, Walridge, Walderige and Waldrugg. The village is mentioned in the Domesday book, with various transfers of land between John Pykoc and Robert Pykoc in 1310. The Steward of the Bishop of Bayeaux held Waldridge as an under-tenant in 1086.

REFRESHMENTS:
The Shoulder of Mutton Inn, Owlswick.

Maps: OS Sheets Landranger 175; Explorer 3.

Some reasonable peace and quiet can still be found close to the motorway on this hilly walk either side of the M40.

Start: At 786926, opposite the Old Ship Inn on the road between Lane End and Stokenchurch.

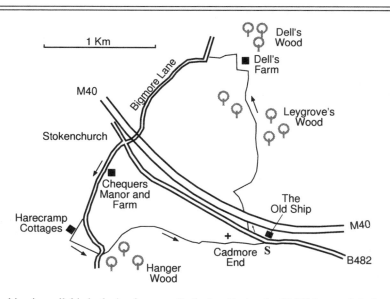

Parking is available in the lay-by opposite the inn. Facing the Old Ship, turn left along the main road (the B482), cross, with care, and turn right along a path just beyond the telephone and post box. The path winds through the wood towards the motorway. Go down some steps and through the tunnel beneath the motorway, continuing along a wide track for a further 150 yards before turning right by the footpath marker post. Go down hill to reach a tarmac track. Turn right to the valley bottom and, just before the gap in the trees, turn left over a stile and cross the narrow end of the field beyond to enter Leygrove's Wood. Go uphill through the wood to reach a track. Turn left, still going uphill. Now ignore the first crossing path, but at the next, continue basically ahead by bearing left along path S51. Continue ahead at the next crossing path, tackling a short uphill stretch to emerge on to open farmland. Keep to the right-hand edge of a field and turn left in the corner, walking along the boundary of Dell's Farm.

At the end of the fence, turn right along a wide track with the farm on your right. Do not cross the stile ahead: instead, turn left down a concrete track and, at the junction with Bigmore Lane, turn left along the lane, soon passing the entrance to **Gibbon's Rare Breeds Centre**. Continue along the lane, crossing a bridge over the motorway, to reach the B482. Turn right and, after 30 yards, cross, with care, and turn left down Chequers Lane, passing Chequers Manor and Farm. Where the lane levels out and bears left, bear right, still going downhill, towards Harecramp Cottages. There are good views from here across to Ibstone House, on the right. After passing the farmhouse, turn left over a stile before two sets of double metal gates and bear left across the field beyond, heading for a small stand of trees. Cross a stile and a lane to reach the woodland footpath opposite, following it with a fence on your left. Ignore a path joining from the right, continuing ahead, uphill. On leaving the wood, turn right to go through two gaps in field corner. As you reach the top of the hill, **Cadmore End Church** can be seen diagonally to the left. Turn left at the T-junction and go past a small pond on the left. On reaching the church, turn right along a rough track, passing between rows of cottages to reach the main road and the start.

POINTS OF INTEREST:

Gibbon's Farm Rare Breeds Centre – The Centre is a farm using traditional working methods together with a rare breeds collection. The Centre is ideal for children who can pet, stroke and feed the animals. There is a tea room, and accommodation is available. The Centre is open all year.

Cadmore End Church – Dedicated to St Mary-le-Moor, this plain, aisleless country church with an open timber porch and big tiled roof was built in 1851. The stained glass windows are dated 1855 and 1884.

REFRESHMENTS:
The Old Ship Inn, Cadmore End.

Maps: OS Sheets Landranger 176; Explorer 3; Pathfinder 1158.
Level walks through two country parks.
Start: At 005833, the car park at the Black Park Country Park.

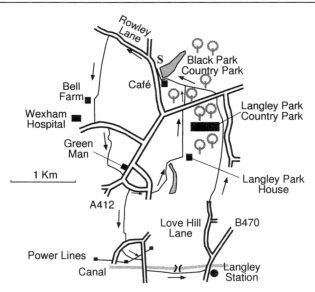

Turn right along the road and, after 60 yards, bear left along Rowley Lane. After 10 yards, turn left along a signed bridleway running parallel with Rowley Lane. At the end of the wood, turn left down Galleons Lane, following it for about a mile, passing a golf course and Bell Farm, on the right. Go over a crossing path and continue, with Wexham Hospital on your right, to reach a lane. Turn left, then, after 250 yards, turn right through a hedge gap, and immediately right again through a gate. Go along a wide grass track between fences, ignoring a turn to the right. At a T-junction, turn left – the footpaths have been re-routed in this area following the development of the gravel pits on the left. Just before reaching the stable blocks, turn right over a stile and head for the left field corner to reach the A412 between the Green Man Inn and a garage. Cross, with care, and go down George Green Road.

The shorter walk follows the road to Coronation Avenue. Cross, and keeping to the left of George Green Lodge, enter **Langley Park**. Follow the gravel track around the lake to reach the main drive to Langley Park House. Turn left up the drive to reach the A412 again. Cross, with care, and bear right along the track into Black Park. At the first crossing path, turn left to reach a lake. Turn left, passing the toilets and café, and following the lake around to reach a walkway back to the starting car park.

The longer walk turns right after 100 yards following Westfield Lane. Cross a stile and continue between hedges. At the end of the path, cross a stile and go down a short drive to a lane. Turn right and, after 200 yards, turn left over a stile to reach a stone stile beneath the two pylons. Keep to the left field edge and cross a stile on to a lane. Turn right, go over the canal bridge and turn right down an angled path. Turn right along the towpath to go back under the bridge. At the second bridge, leave the towpath, turning left along the road. Cross the canal and, after 80 yards, turn left down Trenches Lane. Where the lane bears right, bear left along Love Hill Lane. Bear right at the lodge, turning left before the next pair of gates to continue ahead with a wall on your right. Langley Park House can be seen to the left. Ignore a path on the left, crossing a stile on to a wide grass track. The track narrows: cross a stile and continue with a wall on your right. At the end of the wall, bear left through a gap into Langley Park. After 20 yards, turn right through a horse barrier on to a wide track. Go past a car park and continue through the rhododendrons. Now stay on the main path, going generally north and passing a group of 800 year old yew trees, to reach the A412. Cross, with care, to the horse barrier opposite, entering **Black Park**. At a three-way fork, take the left path (Beeches Way), following it over two crossing paths to reach the short walk at a lake, following it for the last few steps back to the start.

POINTS OF INTEREST:

Langley Park – The Park covers an area of 500 acres and dates back to the 15th century. It was originally a Royal Manor, the house being built in 1740-55 by Charles, the second Duke of Marlborough, as a residence nearer to London than Blenheim Palace. Much was replaced with artificial stone during restoration in 1983/4. The park was landscaped by Capability Brown in 1763/4.

Black Park – The Park is an attractive woodland area of some 500 acres. There is a lake, a nature trail, and swimming and boating facilities.

REFRESHMENTS:

The Green Man Inn, on the A412.
A café is open all year round in Black Park.

Maps: OS Sheets Landranger 166; Pathfinder 1095.
Pleasant field paths and minor lanes to the south of Flamstead.
Start: At: 078145, St Leonard's Church, Trowley Hill Road,
Flamstead.

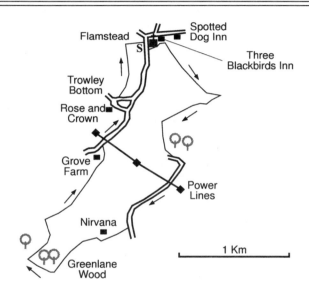

Continue down Trowley Hill Road and, after passing Pound Cottage, turn left into the churchyard. Leave through the gate to join a lane. Turn right, and immediate left opposite the village hall. Follow the lane around to the right and, soon, take the signed path on the left, following it between houses to reach a kissing gate. Go through and turn right along the field edge. The rumble of the M1 motorway can be heard from the left. Follow the path downhill and, on reaching the hedge corner, continue ahead across the centre of the field. Go through a kissing gate and bear left to reach a gate in the corner. Turn right along a wide bridleway, following it around an S-bend and continuing ahead along a narrower section which can get quite muddy. Continue along a fenced path and go through a gap to reach a wider path. At a T-junction with a waymarker post, turn left along an uphill path. If the gate is closed, go over the stile to continue ahead, passing a small wood on the left. At a waymarker post, bear left across the field to pass a single oak tree. Cross a stile and, at the bridleway, turn right to reach a minor lane. Bear left to go under the power cables and follow the lane around a left bend.

Now, just before a footpath waymaker post on the left, turn right along a gravel bridleway, passing 'Nirvana'. Where the track bears right, turn left along a path across a field. At the waymarker post, continue ahead to the bottom of the valley. Turn right here, keeping Greenlane Wood on your right. Ignore a path on the left, go through a gap in the fence and turn right, uphill, through the lightly wooded area. Bear right just before the top and cross the centre of a field. Follow the path to the left at the crest of the hill and, on reaching a bridleway, turn right. Bear left at a fork, heading for the storage barns. Pass the barns on your left, continuing downhill to pass Grove Farm. The stumpy tower and spire of Flamstead church can now be seen on the skyline. In the farmyard, bear left at a fork to reach a minor lane. Turn right, ignoring a lane joining from the right to continue into Trowley Bottom. Bear left at the fork and, opposite the Rose and Crown Inn, turn right up Trowley Hill Road. After 100 yards, turn left along a footpath, keeping right of some garages to join a path following the field edge. Turn left at the waymarker post (still following the field edge) to reach a grassy area on the right. Go through a barrier and follow a narrow path back to the start in **Flamstead**.

POINTS OF INTEREST:

Flamstead – There was probably a settlement here in Roman times, and the village was certainly a place of sufficient importance in Saxon times to have its own chapel. The almshouses opposite the Three Blackbirds Inn were given to the village by Thomas Saunders in 1669 and are still maintained by the charity he set up for them.

The oldest part of St Leonard's Church is the tower, which dates from the 12th century. The first known vicar was Thomas de Bassington who was appointed in 1223. The nave is 13th-century, with other parts dating from the 14th and 15th centuries. The church is best known for its medieval wall paintings, claimed to be the best in Hertfordshire. They were discovered in 1929 under layers of plaster.Three well-worn gravestones in the churchyard bear a skull and crossbones, showing that the village was affected by the Plague in 1604.

REFRESHMENTS:
The Three Blackbirds, Flamstead.
The Spotted Dog, Flamstead.
The Rose and Crown, Trowley Bottom.

Walk 30   **ALDBURY**   4m (6km)

Maps: OS Sheets Landranger 165; Explorer 2.

Leave the pretty village of Aldbury to explore Aldbury Nowers along a section of the Ridgeway path.

Start At: 965125, the Greyhound Inn, Aldbury.

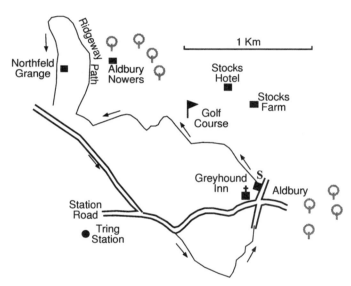

Parking is available in an area close to the inn, which lies in the centre of the village. Take the tarmac path at the side of the Greyhound Inn and bear right to go over a stile. Cross a playing field to reach a stile in the top right corner, cross and bear left across a large field, passing between two trees. Cross a stile in the corner and, at the crossing bridleway, turn left. Just before this left turn **Stocks Hotel** can be seen ahead. Turn right over a stile and follow the path beyond across the golf course. Cross a stile and a crossing track, maintaining direction with a hedge on your left. After 150 yards, ignore the first track on the left, but take the second, which is signed as a footpath. After 400 yards, turn right at a marker post and go through a gap in the fence before a wood. Turn left following the path around, then at the bend, go through a kissing gate on the right to enter the wood, soon going downhill. Ignore a path joining from the left and continue ahead to reach a Ridgeway National Trail marker post. Turn right up steps and, at the top, bear left, following the Ridgeway acorns for about $\frac{1}{2}$ mile. As you reach the top of Aldbury Nowers (one of the best sites for butterflies in Hertfordshire), the Pitstone chalk pits and works can be seen on the left, and there are good views to the reservoirs at Marsworth. Leave the wood through a kissing gate and turn left, downhill, leaving the Ridgeway Trail.

Go over a stile and continue ahead. Turn left over another stile and follow a wide bridleway, with Aldbury Nowers on your left. Go over a pair of stiles and, after a few yards, turn right along a gravel track, keeping Northfield Grange on your left. Go past a white cottage and continue to reach a crossing path, just after the gate posts to the grange. Turn left along this bridleway, going uphill. Go through two gates and turn right down a track. Continue downhill, passing the Wildlife Trust notice board, then go through a horse barrier to rejoin the Ridgeway National Trail. Turn left at the crossroads, still following the Trail. Tring Station can be seen on the right. At the crossing path, leave the Ridgeway, continuing ahead to reach Station Road. Turn left and, at the sharp left bend, turn right along a footpath. Go over a crossing path, continuing with a hedge on your left. The village of **Aldbury** can now be seen on the left. Cross an all-weather horse track and, after 60 yards, turn left over a stile, heading for the village. Continue along a road to reach the main village road. Turn left, passing the Valiant Trooper Inn to reach the village centre.

POINTS OF INTEREST:

Stocks Hotel – This beautiful 18th-century house has been renovated and is now a smart hotel and country club. It was owned from 1851 to 1920 by Mrs. Humphrey Ward, a well-known novelist and one of the first lady magistrates. George Bernard Shaw was an occasional guest at the house. The house was owned more recently by the chief executive of the London Playboy organisation.

Aldbury – This fairly large village has its prettiest and most attractive houses situated around the village green, which has been a background for many cinema and television films. The village pond, old stocks and whipping post are situated at one end of the triangular green.

The village church, of St John the Baptist, is an ordinary, early English building, but with a splendid stone screen guarding the Pendley chapel and its monument to Robert Whittingham and his wife, dated 1452.

REFRESHMENTS:

The Greyhound Inn, Aldbury.
The Valiant Trooper, Aldbury.

FINGEST

4m (6km)
or 10m (16km)

Maps: OS Sheets Landranger 175; Explorer 3.
A real test of stamina on the ups and downs of the Chiltern Hills.
Start: At 777912, Fingest Church, opposite the Chequers Inn.

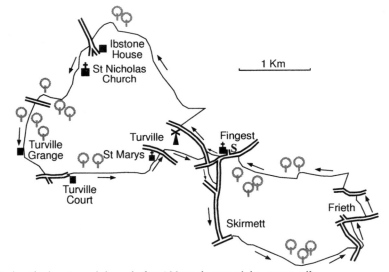

Facing the inn, turn right and after 100 yards, turn right, over a stile.

For the shorter walk: on reaching a wood, turn left at the three-way fork and then left again along a lane. At a T-junction cross the road and then a field corner. Cross two stiles on to a lane, and bear right into Skirmett. Go past the Frog and the Old Crown inns and, where the lane bears right, turn left along a narrow lane. Go past the Stud Farm and turn right, uphill, along a bridleway. Enter a wood and bear right, uphill. Bear left at a fork, go through a new plantation and leave the wood along a fenced path. Cross a road and immediately turn left over a stile. Before the next stile, turn right along the field's left edge. After 250 yards, turn left over a pair of stiles. Cross a road by Frieth Church on to a wide track. Cross two stiles, turn left at a lane, and then right by a post box. At a crossing track, continue into the wood. Bear left and, at a prominent crossing path, turn left. After a left bend, turn right along a wide track to leave the wood. Bear right at a fork and right again to a marker post, entering Fingest Wood. Cross the **Fieldfare stile**, turn left and go downhill along the field's left field to reach a road. Turn left to return to the start in **Fingest**.

The longer walk turns left, uphill, at the three-way fork. Cross a stile and turn right along a lane. Opposite a cottage with a **Windmill** behind it, turn right along a footpath. At a crossing fence, turn left over a stile and go downhill. Leave the wood, bear right to a stile and immediately turn sharp left along a bridle way, following it for over a mile, ignoring a path (LE46) on the right. Cross a stile into a wood and, before reaching a storage barn visible through the trees, turn left, uphill, along a bridle way. At a crossing track, turn left, then bear left to follow an uphill path to a road. Turn left, passing Ibstone School. Ibstone House is on the left by the road junction. Turn right, by the junction into a wood. Bear left and then turn left at a crossing path. Ignore a path to the left (to St Nicholas' Church) and continue downhill. Ignore a track on the left, continuing along a narrow path. Cross a stile and turn left, crossing two stiles to enter a wood. Go over a concrete track, then turn right at a T-junction. After 150 yards, bear left to a road. Cross to an uphill path towards Idlecombe Wood. Cross a stile, turn right, and then immediately left, uphill. Ignore all turnings, crossing a stile to leave the wood. Cross the centre of a field, with Turville Grange on your right. At the hedge line, turn left and cross a stile on the right, following the left edge of the next field. Bear right to a lane and turn sharp left (Turville Court only). Opposite the Court, go through a gap and gate and turn right. Go through a gate and keep to the right of the wood. Bear right at the corner and turn left at the crossing path into Turville. On reaching St Mary's Church, turn right (near the Bull and Butcher Inn) and immediately left. Cross the right-hand stile, bear right into the wood and, at a lane, turn right to rejoin the shorter walk.

POINTS OF INTEREST:
Fieldfare stile — The stile was built in memory of Henry Bridges Fearon 1907-1995 who compiled walks in the Chilterns, under the name of Fieldfare, for several publications including the London Evening News.
Fingest — St Bartholomew's Church is one of the most interesting in the county. It is Norman in origin with a 30 foot square tower and walls 3 feet thick. The unusual twin-gabled, saddle-back roof with elaborate carved openings to the belfry is a later addition.
Turville Windmill — This Copstone Mill dates from the 18th century and was the family home in the film *Chitty-Chitty Bang-Bang*.

REFRESHMENTS:
There are inns in Fingest, Skirmett and Turville, as mentioned in the text.

Maps: OS Sheets Landranger 165; Explorer 2.

A climb to the south of Tring, joining a section of the Ridgeway Path, and a steep descent into Tring Park on the return.

Start At: 925111, the Walter Rothschild Zoological Museum at the end of Akeman Street, Tring.

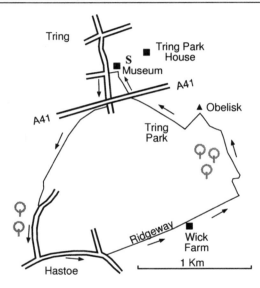

Leave the **Museum** entrance and turn left to reach a T-junction. Turn right, and immediately left down Hastoe Lane, which is signed for Chesham. Go under the main A41 road and turn right through a kissing gate, going uphill along a concrete track. Continue along the right edge of a field, above the A41, and, on reaching a metal gate, bear left to continue uphill, soon walking with a hedge on your left. Go through a gap in the hedge, continuing ahead into Stubbings Wood. Go through a gap, with the wood now on your right and, at the next gap, enter the wood and immediately turn left along the wood's left edge. At a fork, bear left, then ignore a path to the right and continue ahead, passing a barn on the left. Drop down to a concrete track and go through a gate to reach a lane.

Turn right, continuing uphill and passing a riding school, to arrive at a T-junction. Turn left along Church Lane, a pleasant lane, which is part of the Ridgeway National Trail, to reach Hastoe Cross. At the crossroads, continue ahead along a gravel track signed as part of the Ridgeway. Go past Wick Farm and, before the next group of houses, turn left over a stile and go along a narrow path. Following the Ridgeway Trail waymarkers along the rear gardens of some houses, then cross a tarmac path and maintain direction to reach a path junction. Here the Ridgeway goes to the right, but you turn left along a wide track. Go over a crossing path, then bear right along a downhill path. At the **Obelisk**, turn left to continue downhill. Leave the wood through a swing gate to enter **Tring Park**. Turn right and, soon bear, left, heading for a footbridge over the A41. To the right here you can see Tring Park House. Cross the footbridge and follow a narrow tarmac path to return to the Museum.

POINTS OF INTEREST:

The Walter Rothschild Zoological Museum – The museum houses the finest collection of stuffed and mounted animals anywhere in the world. Once the private collection of Lord Rothschild, the Museum has more than 4000 species in a unique Victorian setting. The museum is open daily and on Sunday afternoons.

Obelisk – The monument in the woods is said to commemorate the famous Nell Gwynn and her charms. The 300 acre park was purchased by Dacorum Borough Council for the benefit of the town and is ideal for walking. Experimental grazing is conducted in the park in order to stimulate the growth of wild flowers. The cow herd is limited to 40 animals. These 40 roam the park's many, many acres – surely the happiest cows in the country.

Tring Park – The grand house at the centre of the park was designed by Sir Christopher Wren. Charles II entertained his mistress Nell Gwynn here.

REFRESHMENTS:

There are ample opportunities in Tring, particularly in the High Street at the northern end of Akeman Street.

Walk 34   **WARESIDE**   4m (6km)

Maps: OS Sheets Landranger 166, Pathfinders 1096 and 1097.

A climb, north of Wareside, to an ancient moated site, then down into the valley to return along a dismantled railway line, following the River Ash.

Start: At 396156, the car park at the Village Hall, Wareside.

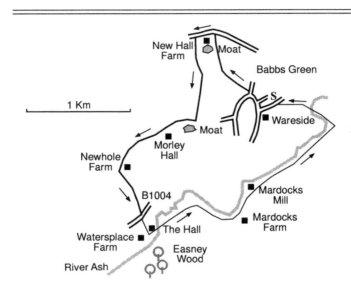

The Village Hall car park lies behind the Chequers Inn. From it, join the main village road and turn right, then right again on a road signed for Babbs Green. Continue until a road joins from the left, then go up steps by the chapel and cross a stile. Cross the centre of the field beyond. The houses of Babbs Green and Holy Trinity Church can be seen on the right. At the hedge corner, continue ahead, walking with the hedge on your left. Cross a stile on the right, at the end of the track, and continue along the left edge. Go past New Hall Farm and through a gate. Cross two stiles and turn left along a road. Go past the farm drive (on the left) and, after a further 50 yards, turn left along a worn concrete track, passing through the farm buildings. The remains of an old moat can be seen to the left. Continue with the hedge on your right, then keep right of the trees in the corner to go through a gap. Follow the path beyond between fields to reach a gravel crossing track. Turn right, soon with **Morley Hall** on your left. Follow the path around to the left, passing a pond. Through the trees on the left, the remains of the moat can be seen in front of Morley Hall. Ignore two paths joining from the right and continue ahead. Cross a stream, using the footbridge if necessary, pass between farms and bear left along a gravel path, soon passing a white bungalow on your left.

On reaching a road (the B1004), turn right and then, immediately, left (crossing with care) to go along a track, passing between Watersplace Farm, on the right, and The Hall on the left. Before a metal gate and a ford, turn left along the dismantled railway, following the River Ash on your right. Cross the river for the second time to bear right at a fork 100 yards before a road bridge. On reaching the bridge, turn right, following the gravel track, with Mardocks Farm to your right. Ignore a turn to the left to cross the river and turn left through a metal gate. Mardocks Mill can be seen to the left. Go through a pair of metal gates and continue ahead, still following the line of the river. After a winding section of river, go over a stile in the corner, by a bridge, and cross the dismantled railway. Follow the path with the river on your left, then cross a footbridge to head away from the river towards the houses at **Wareside**. At the road, turn left: the Village Hall is soon reached on the right.

POINTS OF INTEREST:

Morley Hall – Originally two 17th-century cottages which were joined together and enlarged in the 18th century. The enlarged property was given a new entrance, front and interior in 1956.

Wareside – This is a beautiful village with extensive views from its elevated position above the River Ash and along the Lee valley. On one side can be seen Easney Park with its picturesque mansion above the trees, a fore ground of the village and church of Amwell and, in the distance, the valley towards Cheshunt. Easney Park Wood used to be one of the most celebrated coverts for foxes in the county. The yellowish-brick Holy Trinity Church was built in 1841.

REFRESHMENTS:
The Chequers Inn, Wareside.
The White Horse Inn, Wareside.

Maps: OS Sheets Landranger 165 and 152; Pathfinder 1047.
Passing the impressive Whaddon Hall and the site of a Benedictine Priory.
Start: At 805342, the Lowndes Arms Inn, Main Street, Whaddon.

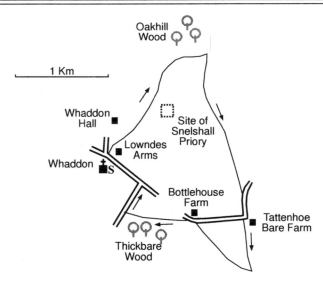

If you use the inn car park, please check with the landlord beforehand. At the rear of this 16th-century inn's car park, cross a stile in the left corner and turn left. Go through a gate, with the grounds of **Whaddon Hall** on your left. Bear right to a stile in a fence, with the Hall now prominent on the left. Go to the right of the pond to reach a stile in a fence. The site of the **Snelshall Priory** is to the right. Go across a field to a stile by a metal gate, keeping to the left field edge. Cross a stile and bear right to a stile into Oakhill Wood. Follow the well-defined path through the wood. Leave the wood through a gate and turn right along the right field edge, following the North Bucks Way. Leave the wood edge on the right to continue with a hedge on your right. Go through a gap and continue ahead, going through a gate on to a gravel track between hedges. Ignore signed bridleways, left and right, continuing along the gravel track. On leaving the track, continue ahead along a lane for about 400 yards. Now, where the road bends sharp right by Tattenhoe Bare Farm, continue ahead along a bridle way. Go through a gap and along a wide grassy track. About 200 yards before the road ahead, turn right along a wide path, crossing a stile and a footbridge and continuing through an area of scrub. At a marker post, bear right across the field then, near the top of the hill, bear left to a stile in the hedge by a horse jump.

Bear right towards Bottlehouse Farm, keeping to the right of the poultry houses, and then to the right of the farm, to cross a stile in a hedge. Turn left along a lane, passing the drive to New Bare Farm and, after a further 50 yards, turn left over a stile and follow the hedge line around to the right. Go through a gate in the corner, over a crossing track and through a gate, following the edge of Thickbare Wood. Go through a gate and bear right to go through a metal gate on to a road. Turn right and, after 250 yards, turn left over a stile and follow a path through the trees. Cross a stile to join a road and turn right. At the T-junction with the main road, turn left into **Whaddon**, following the road past the Congregational Church and the village school. St Mary's Church is behind the houses to the left and the start is just ahead.

POINTS OF INTEREST:

Whaddon Hall – This was the Manor House for many years, and the home of the Lowndes family from 1783. The present Hall is the fourth on the site. The Hall was handed over to the War Office at the start of the 1939-45 War and later occupied by staff from the Foreign Office. It became a factory in the 1960s and a country club in the 1970s. Unfortunately it was gutted by a fire in 1976 and subsequently converted into flats, the outbuildings becoming houses.

Snelshall Priory – Nothing now remains of a small Benedictine house founded in 1166. The stone from the priory was used to build the church of St Giles at Tattenhoe, to the east.

Whaddon – The area around the village was a medieval hunting forest, granted the status of a chase in 1242 by Henry III. At one time the forest covered over 2,200 acres and supported 1,000 head of deer. After timber felling in 17th century and enclosure in 1840, only about 250 acres remained, this being used for fox, rather than stag, hunting by the Whaddon Chase Hunt (now incorporated into the Bicester and Warden Hill Hunt). The village stands high on the edge of a ridge and from the churchyard of St Mary's Church there are splendid views of open and attractive countryside. The church was originally built in 14th century, but restored by JO Scott in 1889/91. The 17th-century clock in the tower is still in working order.

REFRESHMENTS:
The Lowndes Arms, Whaddon.

Walk 36   **WESTON**   4m (6km)

Maps OS Sheets Landranger 166; Pathfinder 1073.

Along undulating field paths through pleasant meadows.

Start At: 258298, in the main street, Weston.

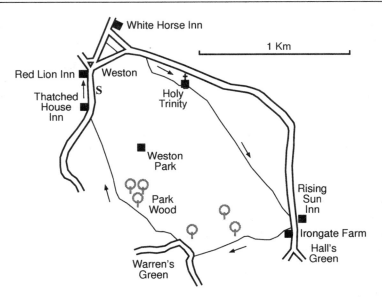

From a point between the Thatched House and the Red Lion Inns, walk northwards along the main street, passing the village green, a pond and some very attractive thatched cottages. Before reaching the White Horse Inn, ahead on the right, turn right, opposite Swaynes Cottage, along a gravel track signed for Maidenstreet. The track soon becomes a fenced path beside gardens: follow it to a road and turn left. Now ignore a path signed for Hall's Green, going downhill along minor road. Pass a school, on the right, and immediately turn right along a drive, At the end of this short drive, continue ahead along a path between hedges. Go over a crossing path and through a kissing gate to enter the churchyard of **Holy Trinity Church**. Follow a path, with the church on your left. Before leaving the churchyard gate, notice the unusual sign on the right, identifying **Jack O'Legs grave**. Go through the gate and turn right. After 10 yards, turn left along a path signed for Hall's Green. Bear right across the centre of a field to a gap in the hedge. Go through a small area of scrub, maintaining direction along a well-defined path, with Bullock's Pasture Plantation on your left. Go through a gap, keeping an intermittent hedge on your right. On reaching a concrete drive, go ahead, across the centre of a field, keeping just right of a telegraph pole. Cross a stile, and bear left to another in the corner. Go through an area of scrub and across a field corner. Cross a stile on to a road and turn right, passing the Rising Sun Inn on the left. Now, before the buildings of Irongate Farm, on the right, turn right along a gravel track. Follow the track to the left, then turn right along a wide farm track. Ignore a track to the right, continuing ahead, soon with a wood on your right. Leave the wood corner, continuing along the gravel track. Go over a crossing path and turn right along a lane. After 200 yards, where the lane bear left, go through a kissing gate on the right and follow the left edge to cross a stile. Bear left to pass an unused stile, then maintain direction to reach a stile to the right of the trees. Cross a field corner, keeping Park Wood on your right. Ignore a path to the left and, at the wood corner, cross a tarmac drive to go through a kissing gate . Go along the left edge of a field, with Weston Park over to the right. Cross a stile in the corner and go through a kissing gate on to a tarmac drive. Turn left and, at the road, turn right to return to the start.

POINTS OF INTEREST:
Holy Trinity Church – The lower part of the central tower and the nave are the remains of a 12th-century cruciform church. The upper part of the tower was added in 1867. Inside there, is a 15th-century piscina and an octagonal font of the same date.
Jack O'Legs Grave – This giant lived many centuries ago in a wood near Weston. He was a highway robber, but very much in the Robin Hood mould, robbing the rich and giving to the poor. Jack had an ongoing feud with the Baldock Bakers who eventually cornered him in the churchyard of Baldock Church. Before he was killed, Jack was granted one last wish that he be buried where his last arrow fell. He fired the arrow straight and true, beyond the churchyard, across the parish of Weston, hitting the tower of Holy Trinity Church. Here the giant was buried, one stone at his head and one at his feet, the two being 14 feet apart. One version of the legend maintains that he even had to be doubled over to get him into the grave.

REFRESHMENTS:
The Thatched House, Weston.
The Red Lion, Weston.
The White Horse, Weston.
The Rising Sun, Hall's Green.

Maps: OS Sheets Landranger 165; Explorer 2.
Easy walks along field paths and canal towpaths.
Start: At 919141, the British Waterways car park opposite the
Anglers Retreat and the White Lion.

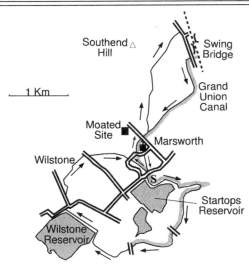

Join the **Grand Union Canal** tow path by the White Lion, then, at the first road
bridge, join the road (Watery Lane). Turn right to the next bridge and rejoin the towpath.
Leave the canal at the next bridge, heading towards Lower End to view the moated
site of Goldingtons Manor with its famous Implement Gate. Return towards the canal,
but before the bridge, turn left to pass a thatched cottage-cum-grocery shop. After a
bend, turn left into a field. Cross a stile by a metal gate, bear left over a stile and
immediately turn right over another stile. Bear left to reach a stile and footbridge and
pass between two wooden posts. The earthworks on the left are the remains of De La
Hay Manor House and its associated village. Bear right along an indistinct path, heading
for a gap in the bushes. Cross a stile and, soon after, a footbridge and head towards
Southend Hill. In the next field bear right, crossing the old **Marsworth Airfield**. Go
over a stile in the corner and cross a concrete area to reach a stile to the right of two

bushes. Bear left over a stile on to a road and turn right. After 100 yards, turn left under a railway bridge and immediately cross a stile on the right. Bear left away from the railway, crossing two stiles and turning right along the towpath. Go past the Pitstone Wharf and shop, and, after passing the thatched grocery shop, go up to the road and turn right into Marsworth. Go past **All Saints' Church**, then turn right and, 150 yards past the Old Manor, turn left along a footpath. Go up a concrete slope to a gate, go through a yard and turn right, through a gate in the corner. Cross a fence using sliding poles to reach a gate and bear left to cross a stile to reach the White Lion.

The longer route now leaves the far end of the car park, following the canal towpath past the reservoirs. At Marsworth Top Lock, double back over the bridge to join the towpath of the little-used Wendover Arm. Cross the bridge to rejoin the towpath on the other bank. Where the canal ends at the Tringford pumping station, walk ahead to reach a road. Cross to a footpath, going down steps and, ignoring a crossing track on the right, head for a pair of stiles in the left corner. Cross and turn immediately right, uphill. Cross two stiles to enter a wood, go over a crossing path and head downhill through the trees. At a junction, turn right along a track. After 150 yards, go left to walk along the side of the reservoir. At the corner, scamper down the bank and turn right along a road. At an S-bend cross to the lane (Tring Road) and, after 150 yards, turn right. Bear left to reach a gate and a tarmac road, then after passing a War Memorial, turn right down Rose Barn Lane. Go over three stiles, eventually joining the canal towpath. Turn right, heading for Marsworth Church, and rejoin the main canal to reach the bridge by the White Lion.

POINTS OF INTEREST:

Grand Union Canal – The canal opened in 1805, the Aylesbury Arm opening in 1815. Startop's End and Marsworth reservoirs were built to prevent an excessive strain on the water supply.

Marsworth Airfield – This war time airfield was first used by Wellingtons, then by American Flying Fortresses and Liberators. The site had an underground bunker, visited several times by Winston Churchill during the later stages of the war.

All Saints' Church – The church was renovated in 1880 by the then vicar, Rev F W Ragg, the work being completed by his own hands with the help of local villagers.

REFRESHMENTS:

The Anglers Retreat, opposite the starting car park.
The White Lion, opposite the starting car park.
The Red Lion, Marsworth.
The Duke of Wellington, Pitstone Wharf.

Walk 39   PIDDINGTON   4m (6½km)

Maps: OS Sheets Landranger 165 and 175; Explorer 3.

Mainly woodland walking, including the Chiltern Society Woodland project at Bottom Wood.

Start: At 806943, the Dashwood Arms, Piddington.

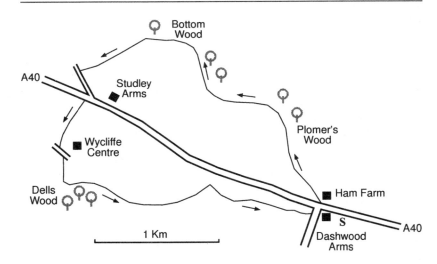

Park in the slip road off the A40. Now cross the road in front of the Dashwood Arms, with great care, bear left and follow a signed bridleway to the left of the buildings of Ham Farm. Turn left through a gate and immediately right along a path between a hedge and a wire fence. After 250 yards, bear right at a fork, going through a gate and heading for another gate into a wood. Follow the well-defined bridleway through the wood, going through a gate and ignoring all turnings. This path can be very muddy after rain.

Go through another gate and continue ahead along the marked path (RA31). Soon, turn right through a gap in the wire fencing to enter **Bottom Wood**. Follow the path to the left, then go through a gap in a fence and continue ahead to reach a wire enclosure fence. Turn left, then immediately right, maintaining direction on a path

78

which winds through very peaceful woodland where many species of birds and animals can be seen. The greater spotted woodpecker is a regular inhabitant. At a path junction at the wood's end, turn right for 10 yards, then turn left on to a fenced path (S72) along the valley bottom. Go through a gate by a timber storage shed and, after 15 yards, turn left along an uphill track between houses and gardens. Go past a high brick wall, bear right to reach a road and turn left along it to reach the A40 by the Studley Arms.

Cross the road, with great care, and turn right to reach a footpath (on your left). At the first crossing path, continue ahead along path S 51 into the heart of woodland. When you leave the wood, ignore a stile on the left, maintaining direction along the Wycliffe fitness trail. Go under an archway of trees to reach the main gates of the **Wycliffe Centre**. Cross the road and follow the path ahead, keeping the buildings to your left. On leaving the last wooden building, re-enter the wood, following the white waymarker arrows to reach a fence. Turn left, then bear right and, when the fence goes to the right, keep ahead, following a waymarked path downhill.

At the bottom of the hill, at a crossing track, turn left along a bridleway (S54) Continue along the valley bottom through Dells Wood. Go through a gate and continue along the edge of the field beyond. Go through a gap in a hedge and, at the corner of a wood, bear right, following the track downhill. Bear left at the next stand of trees, heading for a brick and flint cottage to your left. Go past the cottage and continue ahead on a more pronounced farm track to reach a lane. Turn left and then right to reach the Dashwood Arms and the start.

POINTS OF INTEREST:

Bottom Wood – The wood was given to the Chiltern Society in 1983 to be managed as a nature reserve. It has an area of 36 acres, 28 acres of ancient woodland with many varieties of trees and shrubs and the 8 acres of Toothill planted in 1951 with Scots pine and beech. 'Toothill' is Anglo-Saxon for a lookout or watch place. Old saw pits are common in the wood and demonstrations of the two man saw and the pole lathe are occasionally organised by the Chiltern Society.

Wycliffe Centre – The Centre, at Horsleys Green, and its sister organisation the Summer Institute of Linguistics were founded in America and named after John Wycliffe the first translator of the Bible into English. As well as being a language school, the Centre is involved in 650 Bible translation projects around the world.

REFRESHMENTS:

The Dashwood Arms, Piddington.
The Studley Arms, Studley Green.

Walk 40   **BURNHAM BEECHES** $4^1/_2$m (7 km)

Maps: OS Sheets Landranger 175; Explorer 3.

A walk through beechwoods to Littleworth Common.

Start: At 957851, at Farnham Common, in Lord Mayors Drive.

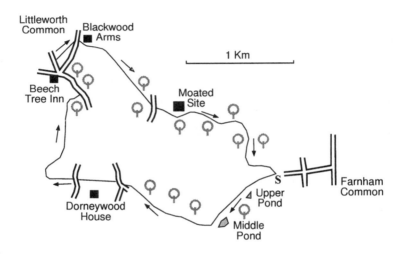

At Victoria Cross, bear left and pass behind the wooden shelter, following the path into the wood. At a wire fence, turn right, with the fence on your left, to reach Upper Pond. Maintain direction, ignoring a fork to the right, to reach Middle Pond. (Until 1883 these ponds were used for washing sheep.) Turn right to cross a grassy area, bearing right to see Druids Oak, at 450 years old the most ancient specimen in **Burnham Beeches**. Cross the road by a speed hump to reach a path and a wooden fence. Do not enter the fenced area: instead, follow the fence and, where it goes right, turn left, passing a typical example of a pollarded beech. Ignore a left fork, continuing downhill to the valley bottom. Turn left along a gravel track and, at a crossing path, turn right, soon going uphill. At a junction of paths, continue ahead, leaving the main track, to join a narrower path. As the trees thin out, take any of the paths ahead to reach a road. Turn right, cross the road, then go left along a signposted footpath. Cross a stile and follow the left edge of a field. **Dorneywood House** can be seen on the left. Cross a stile, a road and another stile, heading for the left edge of a group of trees. At this corner, turn immediately right and cross a stile. Go between holly bushes into a field. Now ignore a stile on the right, crossing a stile into the next field. Go through a gap by some oak trees and turn right along the field edge. In the far corner, cross a stile on to a road. Turn left into Littleworth Common, passing the Beech Tree Inn on the left.

Just beyond Common Lane, turn right along a footpath below a line of cables. At a junction of wires, cross a car park by the Blackwood Arms Inn, then, to the right of 'Woodside', take a footpath signed as part of the Beeches Way. Cross two stiles into a paddock and follow the right edge downhill. Cross a pair of stiles and bear right, heading for a gate into Dorney Wood. Follow the well-defined path to reach a road. Cross and follow a path between the rhododendron bushes to reach Morton Drive. Turn left into McAuliffe Drive, a tarmac road. On the left are the remains of the moated site of **Hartley Court**. At a T-junction, leave the road to continue ahead along a path going downhill. Cross a stream and continue uphill. Now ignore a crossing path, but at the next crossing path, turn left, downhill, passing a marshy pond. Follow the path uphill and, where a significant path crosses, turn right, uphill, passing some rhododendron bushes to reach a road. You are now back at Victoria Cross: turn left down Lord Mayors Drive to return to the start.

POINTS OF INTEREST:
Burnham Beeches – This is possibly the oldest surviving managed woodland in the country. Pollarded beech were cut at 8ft high to provide fuel. This form of cutting was used, as opposed to coppicing (cutting at ground level), to keep the new shoots out of reach of livestock and deer. The Beeches was purchased by the Corporation of London in 1880 as an open space for recreation.
Dorneywood House – The House was built in the early 20th century on a site previously occupied by an old farm house. It was left to the nation by Lord Courtauld Thompson for use by government ministers, normally the Chancellor of the Exchequer.
Hartley Court Moat – This 13th-century medieval moated farm consisted of two enclosures, the inner ($1^1/_2$ acres) secured by a rectangular moat as protection from livestock and deer. The outer (9 acres) was secured by a ditch and bank. This can be seen by the speed hump in McAuliffe Drive.

REFRESHMENTS:
The Beech Tree Inn, Littleworth Common.
The Blackwood Arms, on the east side of Littleworth Common.

Maps: OS Sheets Landranger 164; Pathfinder 1070.
An easy walk along field paths to the south of Twyford.
Start: At 664263, the Post Office, Church Street, Twyford.

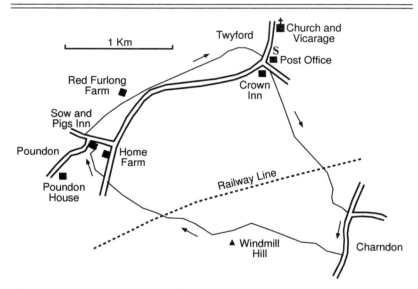

Return to the main road and turn left down Portway Road, opposite the Crown Inn. After crossing a small stream, turn right though a metal gate, following the line of rear gardens. Maintain direction, going through a gate and continuing along the left edge of a field edge to another gate. After 20 yards, turn left, crossing a fence and turning right along a field edge. (Rosehill Farm, marked on some maps, has long since gone.) Go over a crossing track and bear left across the field corner. Go through a hedge gap and turn left. Now, just before the field corner, go over a stile and cross the railway. Cross a stile and the field corner, heading for a dead tree, then follow the hedge line on the left to reach a crossing track. Turn left and, just before reaching a road, turn right over a stile, crossing the field corner to reach a metal gate. Bear right along the main street of Charndon. Ignore a path on the right and, after passing the United Reform Church and the house 'Westdale', turn right over a stile and cross to the gate opposite. Turn left along the field edge to reach a stile. Do not cross: instead, turn right, keeping the hedge on your left. Maintain direction over a stile in the corner, then cross a pair of stiles to the right of the corner, bearing left up the flank of Windmill Hill. Maintain direction downhill, ignoring a stile to the right as you continue towards a marker post. Walk with a hedge on your right to cross a footbridge and a stile, and, soon, bear left to go through a swing gate. Turn right, following the hedge on the right. Go through a gap and bear slightly left to cross a stile hidden behind trees. On reaching the railway line, turn left and, after 10 yards, cross the line and a stile. Bear right across the field corner, go through a gate and cross a footbridge. Now bear left to reach the top of the hill. Go downhill, heading for the field corner and go through a gap (the hedge is on your left). Now head for Poundon, with Home Farm on your right. Cross a road and go through a metal gate to reach a stile. Bear right to another stile, then, with the houses on your left, head into the field corner below Home Farm to cross a stile on to a minor road. Turn left passing the Sow and Pigs Inn at **Poundon**. Continue along the road and, after 30 yards, turn right over a stile at a water pumping station. Turn right and, after 200 yards, turn right over a pair of stiles, bearing left to reach a pair of stiles in a hedge. Bear right towards Red Furlong Farm, crossing a stile just to the right of the field corner. Cross a track and a stile, and bear left away from the road, heading for the four prominent trees in the hedge. Cross a stile and bear left across a field corner to reach a pair of stiles. Bear right, heading for the tower of **St Mary's Church**. Cross a stile and head towards the somewhat derelict farm buildings. Go through the farmyard to reach a lane and turn right to return to the Post Office.

POINTS OF INTEREST:

Poundon – The very handsome Poundon House, at the end of the main street, was built in 1908 for JPH Heywood, the Lonsdale MP. It is of ironstone, in Queen Anne style, and has an H-plan. The Venetian staircase window, somewhat upsetting the balance of the house, can be seen from the road.

St Mary's Church, Twyford – The 14th/15th-century church tower overlooks the remains of a medieval preaching cross and there is a splendid two storey, 15th-century porch with a superb Norman doorway, the door still swinging on its original hinges. The church houses many old brasses, one of which has been used twice. Originally engraved in 1416 for William Stortford, it was re-engraved in 1550 with the portrait of Thomas Gifford we see today.

REFRESHMENTS:

The Crown Inn, Twyford.
The Sow and Pigs Inn, Poundon.

Maps: OS Sheets Landranger 165; Explorers 2 and 3.
A reasonably level walk to the north of Little Missenden.
Start: At 921989, Little Missenden Parish Church.

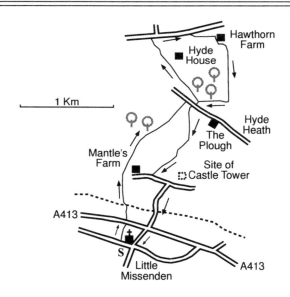

Parking is available on the road opposite the church. Facing the church, turn left, and then right over a stile at the end of the churchyard wall. Keep to the right edge of the field, cross the wooden footbridge over the River Missbourne and a stile on to the main A 413. Cross, with great care, to reach a stile and follow the well-defined path beyond uphill. At the top, go through a gap in the hedge and cross a railway bridge. Turn left at a horse barrier and follow a path into a wood. Now, ignore a track to the left, continuing along the woodland edge and passing Mantle's Farm on the right. Ignore a path on the left, continuing ahead to go through a clearing sometimes used for wood storage. Leave the wood, remaining on the track, with a hedge on your right, then cross a stile on to a road. Turn right and, after 70 yards, turn left along a marked footpath. Just before 'The Paddock', turn left along a footpath into the trees. Bear right on reaching a hedge and walk with the hedge and fields to your left. Go through a gate and continue along a track between houses. After 100 yards, bear left at a footpath marker to enter woodland. On reaching a road turn right, going past Little Hundridge Lane, on the left, and the drive to **Hyde House** on the right. After another 200 yards, cross a stile on the right, by a farm track. Keep to the left of a pair of fenced trees, heading for the barn to the left of Hawthorn Farm. Go through a gate and continue along a concrete track. At the end of the farmhouse garden, turn right over a stile, following the line of the brick wall. Cross a stile to continue along the concrete track.

Go through a gap in the field corner and, ignoring a path to the left, continue towards some cottages. Bear right at the cottage and, opposite a holly bush, take a path on the right to Hyde Heath Common. Bear right at a fork, with fields on your right, then ignore a path joining from the right by a fallen tree and continue ahead. About 30 yards after passing a sports pavilion, turn left at a footpath marker sign and follow the path beside the common, soon reaching a road. To the left here you will see the Plough Inn, **Hyde Heath**.

Turn right and, after 20 yards, turn left down Bull Baiters Lane. Initially this lane is tarmac, but it soon changes to a farm track, and then to a single footway. Continue for about $^3/_4$ mile, emerging on a track at Mantle's Farm. Turn left along the track to reach a road. Turn left. After 300 yards there is a wooden gate on the left, allowing access to the Castle Tower motte and bailey ancient site. To continue the walk, retrace your steps, then turn left along Chalk Lane, going downhill and passing under the railway to reach the A 413. Cross, with great care, and continue ahead down Taylors Lane into Little Missenden. Turn left at the crossroads: the church is on the left.

POINTS OF INTEREST:
Hyde House – The house was built in the late-17th/early-18th centuries and was known as Hyde Hall in 19th century. It was briefly the home of Issac Disraeli (in 1825/26) who was prominent in London literary circles. His son, Benjamin Disraeli wrote his first novel, *Vivian Grey*, here in 1826.
Hyde Heath – The name derives from the heath belonging to William de Hyde. In the 12th century there was a motte and bailey castle here, although now all that can be seen are the remains of the earthworks, a few feet high.

REFRESHMENTS:
The Plough Inn, Hyde Heath, just off the route.
The Crown, Little Missenden.
The Red Lion, Little Missenden.

Walk 43   **GREAT MISSENDEN** $4^1/_2$m (7km)

Maps: OS Sheets Landranger 165; Explorer 2.

Field paths to the west of Great Missenden.

Start: At 895014, Link Road car park, Great Missenden.

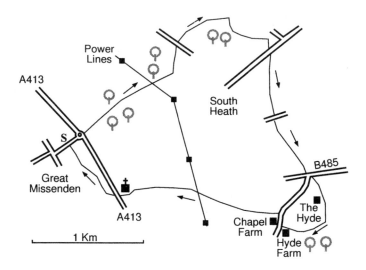

From the car park, turn left towards the main A 413. Keep to the left of the roundabout, cross the road, with care, and go through a kissing gate. Follow a path uphill, cross a stile and continue with a hedge on your right. Go through a gap in the right corner, and ignore a stile on the right, crossing the stile ahead and continuing with a wood on your left. At the wood corner, maintain direction to cross a stile midway between the two electricity pylons. Follow the right edge of the field under the cables and bear left in the corner to cross a stile into the wood. Follow the clearly defined path through the wood, exiting over a stile. Cross the centre of the field beyond, keeping to the right of the stable buildings. Cross a stile, a lane and the stile opposite. Now ignore the path to the left, heading for the right corner of the field. Just before the corner, bear right to cross a stile into a small wood. Keep left of a clearing to reach a double stile in the corner. Cross only the first stile and continue beside the hedge and wire fence on the right. Go past a footpath marker post to reach a stile in the corner of the field (behind the hedge). Cross and turn right over a double stile. Cross the centre of the field beyond and go over a pair of stiles and a field corner to reach a stile by a pair of white cottages. Bear right over a stile, cross a small paddock and another stile on to a road.

Cross the road and take the right-hand path (Marriotts Way), a stony track. Where the track forks, bear right and, after 10 yards, turn left along a path between gardens. Now ignore a path to the right, continuing ahead between hedges and crossing a lane. Maintain direction and cross a stile at the end of the path. Cross the stile in the corner and bear left, away from the wire fence on the right, to cross two stiles on to a road (the B485). Turn left, soon crossing the road, with care, to turn right through the gates of 'The Hyde', passing Hyde Lodge on the right. Walk down the lane to reach the drive into The Hyde. Here, bear left along a footpath between hedges. Cross two stiles, bearing left at the second and, at the valley bottom, turn right, skirting the copse on the left. Cross a stile and immediately turn right along a concrete track, going uphill towards Hyde Farm. On reaching a lane, turn right, passing Chapel Farm. At the next bungalow on the right, bear left along a signed footpath. Keep to the left and cross a stile into a field. Cross a stile and turn left keeping to the field's left edge, to cross a stile in the corner. Cross a stile in the first corner of the next field, maintaining direction and walking with a hedge on your right. Cross a stile in the corner and bear slightly left towards a clump of trees. Cross a double stile and head for **Great Missenden Church**, partly hidden by trees. Go through a kissing gate into the churchyard and bear left over a bridge. Cross the main road, with care, and ignore the steps on the left, following the road down towards Great Missenden. Soon after passing a pair of terraced houses, turn right, then immediately left along a track beside the village school. By the gate into the school playground, bear left and walk through a recreation area to reach a road and the car park.

POINTS OF INTEREST:

Great Missenden Church – The Church of St Peter and St Paul is unusual in that it stands on a hillside away from the village. Dating back to the 14th century, it is largely of flint, but covered in rough cast. It was over restored in 1899 by J O Scott. Inside are several early features – the Aylesbury Norman font with a scalloped base and a 15th-century cup, and some fine brasses.

REFRESHMENTS:

There is a reasonable selection available in Great Missenden.

Walk 44   MEDMENHAM $4^1/_2$m (7km)

Maps: OS Sheets Landranger 175; Explorer 3.

Interesting features all the way along this varied walk.

Start: At 804846, Dog and Badger Inn, Medmenham.

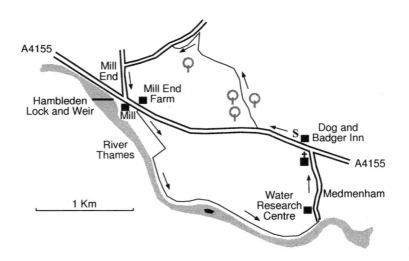

If you use the inn car park, please ask the landlord's permission. From the inn, walk along the A4155 towards Henley, passing the entrance to the Water Research Centre on the left. Just after the **Medmenham** sign, go over a stile on the right and follow a fenced path uphill. At a fork by a waymarker post, bear right, still going uphill. Go past a metal gate and horse jump on the left and a new plantation on the right, then leave the wooded area along the fenced path on the left, ignoring the stile beside it. Go over a farm track and a stile, and turn right along a path beside the wood. At the corner, turn left and, at the sweeping bend of a track, turn left along it, remaining in the wood. On reaching a new plantation, turn right along the signed path, soon going downhill. Go past a pumping station on the right, then cross a stile and follow the right edge of the field beyond. Go over a stile in the corner and turn left along a lane. Cross a bridge over Hamble Brook and, at the T-junction, turn left along the road for Henley and Marlow, following it to the A4155. Cross, with care, turn right and, soon, left between a cottage and a white painted wall. Follow the path to view the mill, Hambleden lock and weir. There has been a mill on this site since 1086: the present mill ceased working in 1952.

To continue the walk, retrace your steps to the main road, and turn right towards Marlow. Go past Mill End Farm, on the left, and some cottages, on the right, then, just before the next set of cottages on the right (dated 1901), turn right down a tarmac track. Turn left along a straight track running parallel with the Thames and follow it until it turns right. There, cross the stile ahead, and immediately turn right along the right edge of a field. In the corner, turn left along the Thames towpath. Follow the towpath for $1^{1}/_{2}$ miles, passing **Culham Court** on the far bank. The towpath ends at a footbridge just beyond the monument commemorating Hudson Ewbank Kearley, 1st Viscount Devonport, who succeeded in proving, in the Court of Appeal in 1899, that Medmenham ferry is public. Ahead is **Medmenham Abbey**. Turn left up a lane, passing the Water Research Centre, on the left, before reaching the many attractive houses of Medmenham. Go past the Church of St Peter and St Paul to reach the main road (the A4155). The Dog and Badger Inn is diagonally left across the road.

POINTS OF INTEREST:

Medmenham – Many fine cottages and houses can be found in Ferry Lane. Two particular fine examples are the 15th-century Manor House and pretty Yew Tree Cottage – note the magnificent sculptured yew hedges. Medmenham Church still retains some of its Norman features, the tower and chancel being 15th-century. The Dog and Badger Inn dates from the 14th century and retains much of its original character.

Culham Court – This Georgian mansion, built in 1770, has terraced gardens running down to the river. The house was substantially restored in the 1930s. George III is said to have visited the house and insisted on having his favourite breakfast rolls delivered from his baker in London. The rolls were kept warm in hot flannels and delivered by a relay team of horses.

Medmenham Abbey – The abbey was founded in the 13th century for a Cistercian brotherhood. The ruins are in fact a clever folly – probably built by Sir Francis Dashwood who purchased the house in the mid-18th century. The builders created the clever illusion by using stone from the ruins of the original abbey. The house became famous as the headquarters of the Hell Fire Club whose members were called the Monks of Medmenham.

REFRESHMENTS:
The Dog and Badger Inn, Medmenham.

89

Maps: OS Sheets Landranger 165; Explorer 2.

An interesting short walk through lovely beech woods to the north of Buckland Common.

Start: 921069, the small lay-by just passed the Horse and Hounds, an inn now converted to a private residence.

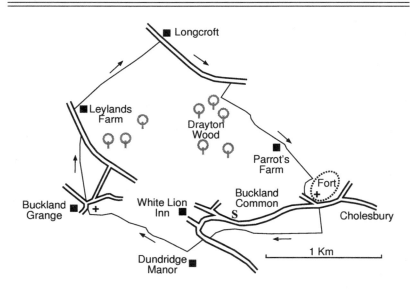

Turn right along the road and bear left up Springall Hill. At the T-junction, with the White Lion on the right, bear left down Oak Lane. Go through the gates to Dundridge Manor, on the left, and follow a tarmac track. Opposite the drawbridge to the original moat, turn right through a wooden gate. Bear left across the small paddock, cross a stile and follow a prominent path through two fields and a playing field. Leave the playing field over a stile and cross a further stile into a small paddock. Bear left, with the whitewashed church and graveyard on the right, and follow a fenced path to reach the church's parking area. Continue to a road, passing Bucklands Grange on the left. Cross, go over a stile by an electricity unit post and follow a path across the left corner to reach a gap in the hedge. Cross a stile continuing uphill to a stile in the corner.

Cross a farm track and turn left along a lane. Just before reaching Leylands Farm, turn right at a 'Private Road' sign and immediately bear left along a track, keeping the farm buildings on your right. Follow the track, with the line of Grim's Ditch on your left. Ignore a crossing path, continuing ahead to reach a T-junction at Longcroft. Turn right down Shire Lane. Ignore a crossing path, soon passing the gates to Drayton Wood House. After another 200 yards, turn right by a metal gate into Drayton Wood, a splendid example of a Chiltern beechwood. At the wood corner, leave the bridle way, turning left over a stile and following a path just inside the wood. Continue for about $^1/_2$ mile, continuing ahead at a crossing path (Parrott's Farm is on your right). Leave the wood over a stile on the right and keep to the right edge of a field. Cross a stile and follow a path along the wood edge. Cross a stile, go through an area of small trees, then bear left to go through a gap. After 10 yards you will reach the boundary of the **Cholesbury Fort**. Turn right along a sunken path and, at its end, turn right, and immediately left through a kissing gate. **St Lawrence's Church** can be seen to the left. Turn right through the church gates to reach a lane. Turn left and left again at the T-junction. Immediately turn right, with a fence on your right. Cross a stile and go downhill, with the disused **Cholesbury Windmill** to your left. At the valley bottom, cross a stile and turn right to pass an unused stile. Cross a stile and go along the right edge of the next two fields. Ignore a path on the right, continuing along a fenced path. Cross a stile into a paddock, bearing left to reach a stile in the corner. Cut across the corner of the next paddock, then cross a pair of stiles and bear left to reach a stile in the hedge. Cross on to a road and turn right. Go past the gates of Dundridge Manor, continuing down Springall Hill to reach the start.

POINTS OF INTEREST:

Cholesbury Fort – Nearly 600 ft above sea level, this Iron Age hillfort has double ramparts and covers an area of 15 acres. Two old ponds lie within the enclosure – Bury Pond and Holly Pond.

St Lawrence's Church, Cholesbury – The church stands within Cholesbury hillfort. Of interest are the 13th-century nave, the 14th-century chancel, the wooden bell turret and the saddleback roof.. The church was substantially rebuilt in 1873.

Cholesbury Windmill – Built in 1880, the mill has an unusual tower with an Ogee Cap. Originally it had shuttered sails. It ceased to operate in 1916 when it was converted to residential use by the addition of a cottage to the base of the tower.

REFRESHMENTS:
The White Lion, Cholesbury.

Walk 46   STOKE MANDEVILLE $4^1/_2$m (7km)

Maps: OS Sheets Landranger 165; Explorer 2.

From Stoke Mandeville to Bishopstone. Some of the paths are indistinct during the summer and very overgrown.

Start: At 834104, the village school, Stoke Mandeville.

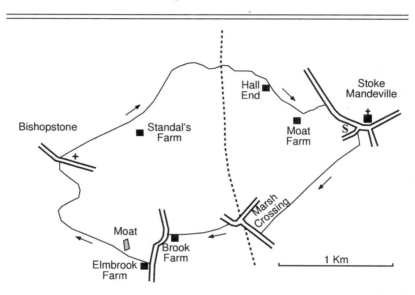

Facing the school, turn left, cross the road and continue along a wide tarmac track. Bear right to remain on the footpath, joining a narrow path between bungalows. Follow this path along the rear gardens, cross a stile and continue with intermittent bushes on your left. Leave the corner of the bushes to cross a footbridge and a narrow field to reach a stile. Continue ahead to cross another stile and turn left to go through a gap in a hedge. Turn right, now with the hedge on your right. Cross a pair of stiles in the corner and the centre of the field beyond. Continue ahead at the hedge corner to go through a gap on to a lane. Turn right, soon turning left, with care, over Marsh Crossing. After 60 yards, turn left along a signed bridleway. Ignore a stile on the left and continue ahead to reach the end of the paddocks on the right. Turn left over a stile, then bear left to cross another stile. Immediately turn right to cross a stile and continue ahead, with a farm on your left. Go through a gap and turn left over a footbridge. Ignore the stile ahead, turning right along a gravel track. At the T-junction, turn left, passing Brook Farm, following the lane around a left-hand bend. Ignore a footpath on the right, turn right up the drive to Marsh Green Cottage and immediately cross a stile on the left. Cross the footbridge (not the stiles) to leave this field. Bear left and, at the corner, with the remains of an ancient moat on the right, continue across the field corner, heading for three prominent trees. Go through a gate and cross a footbridge, to bear left across the field. Cross a metal gate and follow the right edge to a stile. Cross, bear right over another stile and continue ahead. After passing a large storage barn on the right, bear left to go over a stile. Cross a footbridge and the centre of the field beyond to reach a stile in front of **Bishopstone Church**.

Go through a gate to the side of the church, following a fenced path with Old Farm on the left. Cross three stiles and a footbridge, and continue along the left edge. Go through a kissing gate and bear just away from the left edge to go over a stile in the fence. In the top right corner, cross a stile and keep to the left edge to go through a gap. Now ignore the stile on the left and bear right to go through a gap. Turn right to follow a wider track, crossing the railway, again with care. Cross the field between the lines of electric cables and then bear right into the field corner. Now head for **Hall End Farm**. Go through the gate in front of the farm and turn left, passing a small pond. Turn right over a footbridge, then cross a stile at the end of the path. Immediately go left over a pair of stiles and bear right across the corner to reach a pair of stiles. Cross and continue along the left edge of a field. On reaching Moat Farm, to the right, cross a stile and immediately turn left over a stile into a paddock. Follow the path to reach a road. Turn right, passing the Bell Inn to return to the school in **Stoke Mandeville**.

POINTS OF INTEREST:
Bishopstone Church – When the church was built in 1858, several Anglo-Saxon remains were found, including brooches and buckles, pointing to a 6th-century Anglo-Saxon settlement. The remains are now in the County Museum at Aylesbury. Recently the church was converted to residential use and is now known as Chapel House.
Hall End Farm – This 17th-century, timber-framed farmhouse is all that now remains of the hamlet of Stoke Hallinge. Previously there were several cottages and an inn.
Stoke Mandeville – The village is most famous for its hospital which can be seen across the fields. The spinal injuries unit is known across the world.

REFRESHMENTS:
The Bell Inn, Stoke Mandeville
The Bull Inn, on the road to Princes Risborough.
The Woolpack, on the road to Princes Risborough.

Walk 47   GREAT OFFLEY $4^1/_2$m (7km)

Maps OS Sheets Landranger 166; Pathfinder 1072.

An easy walk country lanes and well-signed bridleway, with beautiful scenery all around.

Start At: 143271, the Green Man Inn, Great Offley.

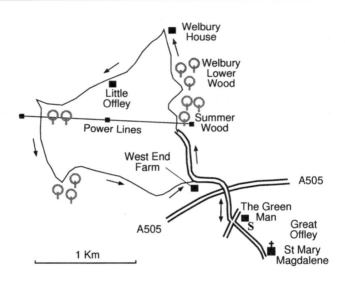

Parking is available in the road close to the inn. From the Green Man Inn, return to the crossroads, with **St Mary Magdalene Church** to the south, and continue ahead, passing the village school and crossing the bridge over the A505. Just beyond the bridge, ignore a footpath on the right, continuing up this quite lane, a 'No Through Road'. Go past West End Farm and around a right-hand bend, ignoring paths on either side. There are extensive views from here over the Hertfordshire countryside. At the fork in front of a pair of cottages, bear right, remaining on the tarmac track. Go under the electricity cables, keeping Summer Wood on your right. Go through a group of houses (following the sign for Welbury House), then bear right to follow the track around the edge of Welbury Lower Wood, now going downhill. Go past a brick house and the wall to Welbury House on the right. Welbury House itself is found behind the bungalows. At the bridleway marker post, turn left across a field to reach the corner of a wood.

Keep the wood on your left, following the well-defined track, soon leaving the wood to go uphill. At the top of the hill it is worth looking back for the views over the parish of Pirton. At the marker post at the top of the hill, continue ahead along a track towards the farm buildings. Go between the two storage barns and a single storey building, keeping the farm house of **Little Offley** – a Tudor manor house – on your left. Go past a wooden gate on the left, and immediately turn left along the left edge of a field. In the corner, follow the track through the wood. On leaving the wood, turn left and then bear right along a track, leaving the wood edge. At a T-junction, turn left along the right edge of a field, ignoring a path on the right, signed for Lilley. Continue ahead under the electricity cables. Soon after the wood corner, ignore the first gap on the left to each a marker post. Here, bear left into the wood. After 200 yards, at a marker post, turn left to emerge into an open area. Continue ahead, beside the wood, and, at the corner, follow the path to the right, soon bearing left across the centre of a field.

Go through a gap and continue along the left edge of a field. Go over a crossing track to continue along the left edge. In the corner, maintain direction along a wide track between hedges. Go past a small pond, on the left, to reach a lane. Turn right and retrace your steps to the Green Man Inn.

POINTS OF INTEREST:

St Mary Magdalene Church, Great Offley – Beautifully situated among the trees of Offley Place. Part of the church – the nave and the aisles – date from 1220. There are also traces of 14th-century glass windows. The chancel was re-modelled in 1750 by Sir Thomas Saulsbury. His elaborate monument is in the south wall. The embattled west tower, with its pyramidal roof rather than the more common Hertfordshire spike, was added in 1800. The greatest treasure is the mid-14th-century font made of Tottenhoe stone. The cover is a fine example of Jacobean carving.

Little Offley – This late Tudor Manor House has an H-shaped layout. There is a fine example of an Elizabethan fireplace inside.

REFRESHMENTS:
The Green Man, Great Offley.
The Prince Henry, Great Offley.
The Bull, Great Offley.
The Lobster Tail, Great Offley is a licensed restaurant.

Walks 48 & 49　　　　**LANGLEY**　　　　4¹/₂m (7km)
　　　　　　　　　　　　　　　　　　　or 6m (9km)

Maps: OS Sheets Landranger 166; Pathfinder 1073.
Woodland paths and passing through Knebworth Country Park.
Start: At 217225, the Farmers Boy Inn, Langley.

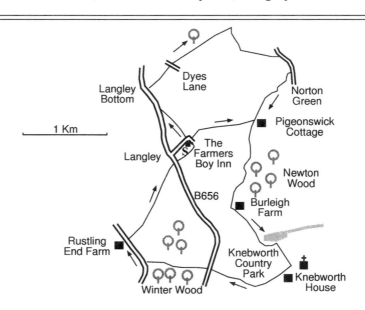

For the short walk, face the inn and turn left, following the track to the right. After 30 yards, turn left through a gate. Bear right along a cattle track. Go through a gate and ignore a path to the left, crossing the field centre towards a white cottage. Turn sharp right along a wide farm track, joining the longer walk.

For the longer walk, with your back to the inn, take the narrow fenced path signed for Langley Bottom. Cross a stile, ignoring a path veering right to cross the field centre. Head left of the oak tree by the hedge corner and go through a gap on to a road (the B656). Turn right, with care, passing a path on the left and, beyond a white cottage, turn right along a bridleway. Bear left beyond a parking area, following a path to the right of a wooden gate. Cross a footbridge and Dyes Lane, following the path opposite. Cross a footbridge by a small pond and bear right along the right field edge, soon going uphill. Go past High Broomin Wood, on the left, and cross Kitching Lane. At an electricity pole, turn right through a gap and go along the left field edge. Follow the path to the left to reach a lane. Turn right. By the Norton Common notice board (the Woodmans Arms, Norton Green, is 50 yards ahead) cross a stile on the right and continue to a stile on to a path along the house rear gardens. In the corner, before the open barn, turn right and in the next corner, bear left though a gap. Turn left at a marker post and go along the left field edge. In the corner, cross a drainage ditch and bear left to a marker post. Go through a stand of trees and cross a stile. Go through a woodyard and bear right along a wide farm track to join the shorter walk.

Follow the track past a new plantation and continue through a wood. Cross a track and leave the wood through a kissing gate. Turn left along a field edge. At the end of the wood, continue with a hedge on the left. Ignore a path to the right and, after 40 yards, turn left over a stile, and head towards Burleigh Farm. Cross a stile and a track, go through a yard and cross a stile into a paddock. Follow a raised path into Wintergreen Wood. Go over two crossing tracks and pass ponds on the left. Bear right and, after 20 yards, cross a steep ladder stile into Knebworth Country Park. Keep to the left edge to reach an avenue of trees. Turn right, between the trees, towards **Knebworth House** and Church. At a T-junction, turn right, passing the house entrance and **Knebworth Barns**. At a fork, bear right along the wider of the tracks. After about 400 yards, where the tarmac track goes left, bear right into a corner and cross a ladder stile on to a road (the B656). Cross, with care, and follow the track opposite through a wood. At a waymarker post, bear right along a narrow path. Go over a crossing track and, at a marker post, bear left to reach a lane. Turn right, ignore the first crossing path, and turn right opposite Rustling End Farm. Bear right into a narrow field and through a gap in its right corner. Follow a wide track for about $^1/_2$ mile to reach the B656 in Langley village. Cross, with care, and follow the track to the right of the Coach House Restaurant. Where the track bears right, go ahead, over a stile and bear right. Cross the fence and go through a paddock. Cross the fence in the corner and turn left along a track to reach the start.

POINTS OF INTEREST:

Knebworth House – In the Domesday Book this was Chenepeworde, the house on the hill. At the beginning of the 19th century three sides of the original house were knocked down and stucco was added to the remaining wing. Sir Edward Bulwer Lytton, the novelist, added the copper domes, gargoyles and further battlements in the middle of the 19th century. The house is open daily during the summer months.

Knebworth Barns – Now a licensed restaurant, but dating from the 17th century. The barns were moved to their present position in 1970 from elsewhere on the estate.

Walks 50 & 51　　　**IVINGHOE**　　　4$\frac{1}{2}$m (7km)
　　　　　　　　　　　　　　　　　　　　or 9m (14km)

Maps: OS Sheets Landranger 165, Explorer 2.
Two loops or one long walk from Pitstone Hill.
Start At: 955149, the Pitstone Hill picnic site car park.

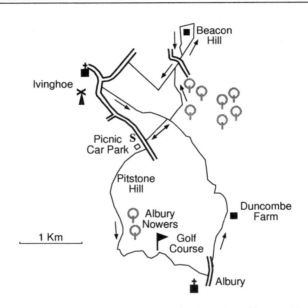

Cross the road, go through a kissing gate and follow the Ridgeway National Trail,
going between fields and through a gate. The track bears left, uphill to a stile. Continue
along a rough track, ignoring a path joining from the right. Go over a crossing path to
a fork and bear left. On emerging from the wood, go ahead towards **Ivinghoe Beacon**.
To the left is the Pitstone Windmill. Follow the track downhill to a lane. Cross and
follow the right-hand track, going over a crossing path and crossing a stile. Bear left
to a stile. Bear left, uphill, and, at the top, turn left, keeping left of a marker post to a
reach stile in a wire fence. Continue ahead, uphill, to reach the trig. point and Ridgeway
map. Now, facing away from the map, follow the worn path ahead, going steeply
downhill to reach a road. Turn right and, after 40 yards, bear left to a stile in a wire

fence. Go steeply downhill and, on leaving the trees, turn left along a crossing path. Join a wider track, cross two stiles and continue with a wire fence on your right. At the end of the hedge, turn right over a stile and bear right to the stile opposite. Cross two stiles and turn left along the road to a T-junction. **Ivinghoe** is to the right. Turn left and, after 30 yards, cross a stile on the left. Cross a broken stile and, at the hedge corner, cross the centre of a field, bearing left to reach a hedge gap. Cross a field corner, then ignore a stile on the left, continuing to the Ridgeway marker post. Turn right to return to the start on Pitstone Hill.

The longer walk continues to the picnic area at the far end of the car park. Cross a stile, then ignore a stile on the right, following the Ridgeway. At a marker post, bear right to a gate, 100 yards from the left corner. Keep to the well-worn path below Albury Nowers and, after 800 yards, bear left down steps. At the marker post, bear right down more steps. Ignore a path on the right, and, at the next post, leave the Ridgeway, turning left, then bearing left at a fork. Go through a kissing gate and across a golf course, heading towards Aldbury. Turn left along a crossing track, and, at the end of the hedge, turn right along a gravel track. Where the track bears left, go ahead, over a stile and along a hedged path. Cross a stile and turn left to reach a lane. Aldbury is to the right. Turn left and, after 50 yards, turn right up steps to a stile. Keep to the left edge and, after 50 yards, turn left over a stile. Cross a farm drive and follow a path beside a cottage. Cross six stiles to reach the drive to Duncombe Farm. Turn left, then, soon, right along a wide track. Cross a stile and bear left, uphill. Soon, bear away from the fence, skirt a small wood on your left and cross a stile. Go along a wide track and, at the top of the hill, bear left along a crossing track. Turn left at a fork. Where the track sweeps left, continue ahead, crossing a stile. Cross a stile by a gate and, after 200 yards, at the Ridgeway marker post, turn left to return to the car park.

POINTS OF INTEREST:

Pitstone Hill – The hill's 54 acres is a designated Site of Special Scientific Interest.
Ivinghoe Beacon – The Beacon, 807 feet high and only 30 miles from London, marks the end of the Ridgeway National Trail and offers superb views. On the top of Beacon Hill is a triangular 6 acre Iron Age hillfort.
Ivinghoe – An interesting thatch hook hangs along the wall in Church Road. Fire was an ever present problem to the thatched homes of the village. This relic, an 18 foot hook, was used to tear the thatch from burning cottages. Beneath it is an iron man trap, an effective way to deal with poachers.

REFRESHMENTS:
None on the route, but available in nearby Ivinghoe.

Walk 52   **WEST WYCOMBE AND BRADENHAM**   4$\frac{1}{2}$m (8km)

Maps: OS Sheets Landranger 165 and 175; Explorer 3.

A ridge walk to view Bradenham Manor.

Start: At 826947, the public car park next to the West Wycombe
Garden Centre, off the A40.

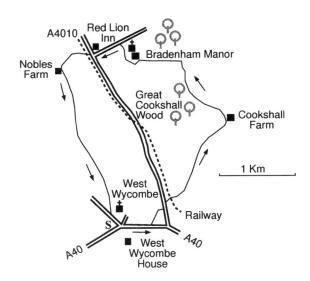

Turn right to the A40 and left along the High Street, passing many of the old timber-faced buildings: the village is now administered by the National Trust. Just past the Rectory, go through a kissing gate and bear right to a field corner. Cross a stile and a road and follow a path to a gate in the far hedge. Go under the railway, cross a stile and go uphill with a fence on your left. Go through a small clump of trees and cross a stile, a track and another stile. Continue uphill, then, just before the barns, go over a fence and cross a yard to join a lane. Follow the lane uphill towards Cookshall Farm. At the top, by a grass triangle, take the footpath to the left. Go through two sets of wooden gates and another gate into the woods. Ignore a track on the left, keeping right to the top of the hill. Cross a track, following the white arrows into Cookshall

Wood. You emerge from the wood by a gate. Do not follow the path uphill: instead, turn right along a grass footpath. Cross the stile to reach a T-junction. Turn left into the wood, following a path to a crossing path. Turn left and, ignoring all turnings, continue to a crossing bridleway. Bear left and emerge at a track and the entrance to Bradenham Hill Farm. Continue ahead, reaching more open ground, and follow the track downhill. Re-enter the wood and, where the track forks, bear right. At a crossing track, turn left and follow the wall of **Bradenham Manor**, on the right, to emerge by the cricket pitch on the common. Bear right, following the wall of the manor to reach Bradenham Church (dedicated to St Botolph and built about 1100).

Cross the road and turn left to reach the A4010 and the Red Lion Inn. Turn right, then immediately cross, with care, to a footpath. Go through a kissing gate and bear right to reach a stile, the railway and another stile, crossing with care. Cross the centre of a field to a gap in the hedge. Cross a stile and walk uphill with a hedge on the left. Cross a stile into woodland and bear left, still uphill, to reach the drive of Nobles Farm. Turn left between the fences and join a grass track between hedges. Go through a kissing gate and maintain direction for $1^1/_2$ miles, ignoring all turnings, to reach the car park at Wycombe Hill. Now head for the gates to the right of the church, go through the churchyard and follow the path to the right. Bear left at a junction, passing in front of the Mausoleum. Take any of the paths downhill, bearing right down steps. **West Wycombe Park** is in front of you and virtually beneath your feet are the **West Wycombe Caves**. Turn right and cross the road to return to the start.

POINTS OF INTEREST:
Bradenham Manor – The estate was acquired by the National Trust (together with the Red Lion, other property, farm land and 380 acres of woods) in 1956. There is a clause in the lease allowing the Village Fete to take place once a year.
West Wycombe Park – The park, mansion and village are the property of the National Trust. The 18th-century Palladian house was built for Sir Francis Dashwood and has fine landscaped gardens containing temples, statuary and a large, swan-shaped lake.
West Wycombe Caves – The caves were dug in 1750 to create jobs for the locals and to provide material for filling the ruts in the London to Oxford Road. The Knights of St Francis, commonly known as the 'Hell Fire Club' regularly met in the caves. The caves are open to the public, the entrance being on West Wycombe Hill Road.

REFRESHMENTS:
The Red Lion, Bradenham.
There are several opportunities in West Wycombe High Street.
There is a tea shop at the Garden Centre.

Walk 53   QUAINTON   5m (7$^1/_2$km)

Maps: OS Sheets Landranger 165; Pathfinder 1070.

A climb to the north of Quainton, with superb views over the Vale of Aylesbury.

Start: At 747202, the Village Green in the centre of Quainton.

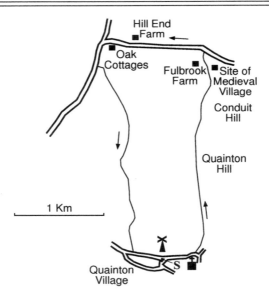

Parking is available beside the Village Green. Walk to the top of the Green, by the **Stone Cross** and, facing **Quainton Windmill**, turn right to pass the village store and, soon, the Almhouses and the **church**. Beyond the church, cross a stile on the left and the small paddock beyond. Cross a pair of stiles and head for the oak trees on the hedge line. In the corner, at the crossing path marker, bear left along a gravel track. Cross the short corner and go through a wooden gate, following the track beyond uphill towards the radio mast. About half-way up the climb, go through a metal gate and maintain direction. On reaching the top of Quainton Hill, look back over the village and the Aylesbury Vale. Follow the track between the mast and a small enclosure of trees, now with good views all around. Go through two gates and, beyond the second, bear right to go down Conduit Hill, heading towards Fulbrook Farm, the red brick farm and out-buildings ahead. At the bottom of the hill, go through a gate just to the right of a dead tree and bear right, keeping to the right of the farm, to go through a gate and small paddock. Go through another gate to reach a track and turn right, following the track to a lane. To the right, here, is the site of a medieval village.

Turn left along the lane, passing a pond and a willow tree on the left. Continue along this little used lane for about $^3/_4$ mile and, after passing Hill End Farm, on the right, and Oak Cottages, on the left, turn left at its junction with another lane. After 300 yards, turn left along a wide farm track, soon crossing a stile on the right and heading for the wood corner by the medieval fish ponds. Keep the circular pond on your right and cross a footbridge, bearing left to reach a pair of stiles in the hedge opposite. Cross and bear right into the top right corner of the field beyond. Go over a double stile and bear right across the corner of the next field. Cross a footbridge and a pair of stiles, maintaining direction, into the top right field corner. Cross a footbridge and bear left, away from the hedge line, heading for an oak tree with a gap in the hedge to its right. In the corner, join a track, but immediately turn left over a stile. Bear left across the field corner and cross a pair of stiles and a footbridge. Go along a path between hedges, then turn right at a crossing path, following it between houses to reach a road. Turn left, then bear left at the fork (along Upper Street) to return to the Village Green at Quainton.

POINTS OF INTEREST:

Stone Cross – This is thought to have been a preaching cross erected in Saxon times before the church was built. The track alongside the Cross is thought to date from the 15th century.

Quainton Windmill – The mill was designed and built by James Antiss, a local man in 1830–2. The tower mill was the tallest windmill in the county and was built from the inside, without scaffolding, using local clay bricks. It was last used in 1881 and is now being restored. It is open to the public on some Sunday mornings.

Quainton Church – Dedicated to St Mary and the Holy Cross, the church has medieval origins, but was much altered and restored in 1870. It is noted for its 17th- and 18th-century monuments to members of local wealthy families, and also has four late 15th-century painted panels of saints. The bells in the tower date from 1621.

REFRESHMENTS:

The George and Dragon, on the Green, Quainton.
There are also other possibilities in the Quainton.

Walk 54   **NEWLAND PARK**   5m ($7^1/_2$km)

Maps: OS Sheets Landranger 176; Pathfinder 1139.

Tracks and field paths to the north of Chalfont St Peter, with two excellent attractions to visit.

Start: At 003935, in a lay-by in Chesham Lane opposite Ashwell's Barn.

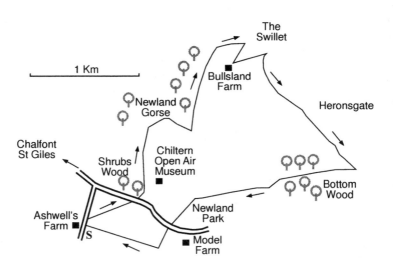

To reach the start, pass Newland Park on your right and take the first turning left. Parking is also available at the Chiltern Open Air Museum or at Model Farm when these two attractions are open. Facing Ashwell's Barn and the very old Ashwell's Farm, turn right and follow the path into the wood. Immediately bear left along a bridleway. At a T-junction, turn right, continuing along the bridleway. Leave the wood and cross a road to the entrance drive of Newland Park and the **Chiltern Open Air Museum**. After a few yards, turn left over a stile and bear right, heading towards the corner of a wood. Leave the wood on your left to follow the left edge of a field. Cross a stile to enter Newland Gorse and bear right, keeping a wire fence on your left. Soon the path is fenced on both side: follow it to the bottom of the valley and bear right along a path to reach Shire Lane. Turn left, uphill, along the stony, sunken track, ignoring all paths which join, and passing Bullsland Farm on your right. About 200 yards after leaving the edge of the wood on the left, turn right along a path signed 'The Swillet'. Bear right on to the higher of the two paths, go through a horse barrier and turn right to reach a track. Turn right and then bear right down Bullsland Lane.

Opposite Bullsland Farm, turn left over a stile and bear left to reach another stile in a fence. Cross and bear right across the field beyond to reach the hedge. Turn right, cross a stile and follow the path beyond along the rear gardens of the houses of Heronsgate. Follow the path over three stiles and, on reaching a projecting hedge corner, turn right, downhill, to reach a metal stile. Go through into Bottom Wood. Turn right at a crossing path and continue to reach open fields on the right. Now turn left along an uphill path. Nearing the top, bear right at a fork (be careful: this can be difficult to spot) and head into the corner of the wood. Leave over a stile and follow the right field edge, crossing a series of stiles to enter Newland Park playing fields. Cross a road and follow a path between fields and an all-weather pitch. Cross a stile by the campus buildings and bear left, keeping just to the right of a clump of trees, to reach a stile in a hedge. Cross on to a road. **Model Farm**, home of the Chalfont Shire Horses, is just down the road to the left. Cross the road and follow a fenced path. After passing some greenhouses, and before reaching a stile, turn right and go over a series of stiles, to reach a path beside a wood. Follow this back to the start.

POINTS OF INTEREST:

Chiltern Open Air Museum – The museum occupies 45 acres of parkland and woodland includes an interesting Nature Trail. Many buildings have been re-erected on the site displaying the traditional building heritage of the Chilterns. The collection grows each year but presently includes barns, stables, cottages, a chapel, a Victorian farm complete with animals, a toll house and a blacksmith's forge. Also of interest is the Hawk and Owl Trust's National Conservation Centre on the museum's village green. The site is open April to October, Tuesday to Sunday and Bank Holidays.

Model Farm – Situated a few hundred yards from the Chiltern Museum, the centre has daily demonstrations with the shire horses and includes a carriage museum, blacksmith's shop, playground and picnic area. The farm is open April to October, Saturday and Sunday, and on weekdays during school holidays.

REFRESHMENTS:

None on the route, but available at the Chiltern Open Air Museum.
Full facilities can be found at Chalfont St Giles, 2 miles to the west.

Walk 55　　　　　DENHAM　　　　5m (7$\frac{1}{2}$km)

Maps: Landranger 176; Pathfinder 1158.

Along a canal towpath, returning through a country park.

Start: At 048863, the car park of the Denham Country Park.

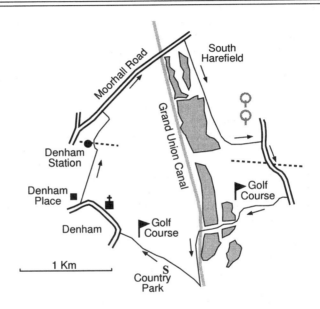

With your back to the Colne Valley Visitor Centre, go through the kissing gate on the side of the golf course and turn left along a path signed for Denham. Pass two small footbridges and continue ahead at a larger bridge to go through a kissing gate on to a road opposite Wellers Mead. Bear right towards the village, ignoring a turning on the right to pass **St Mary's Church**. Maintain your direction to pass the Swan and Green Man Inns and, at the small green in front of the Falcon Inn, bear right, by **Denham Place**, and take the Pyghtle Path. Ignore footpaths on either side, continuing ahead to pass under the railway bridge at Denham Station. Continue ahead, beside the rear gardens of houses and, at a T-junction, turn left to reach the main road (Moorhall Road). Turn right, soon crossing the River Colne. Go past the Horse and Barge Inn, on the right, and cross the canal bridge, with Widewater Lock on your left.

Continue along the road, passing the modern office complex of Widewater Place, and ignoring an entrance into Denham Quarry, then turning right down Dellside. Now ignore a tarmac road to the right, and immediately bear right along a concrete footpath. Cross a stile, as you leave the houses on the left, and maintain direction. Keep a small copse on your left and continue along the right edge of a large field. Ignore a bridle way on the right, crossing a stile in the field corner and going along the left edge of the paddock beyond, passing the Hillingdon Activity Centre on your right. Turn left, then immediately right along a wide track with the Centre's car park on your right. When the fence ends, bear left along a wide track (heavy nettle growth in the summer), go through a gap and follow a path along the right edge of a field. Follow the field edge around to the left, then turn right over a stile on to a road.

Turn right and follow the road for about $^1/_2$ mile, crossing the railway. Take extra care crossing the bridge as there is no footpath. Where the road goes into a shallow dip, turn right over a stile and cross two further stiles into Uxbridge Golf Course. Follow the gravel path across the centre of the course, taking great care. Go through a gap in the trees and, after 30 yards, bear right across the practice area to reach a gap on to an area of scrub. Follow a path between two pair of lakes, go up steps and cross the canal bridge, and turn left along the towpath. Go past Denham Lock, with its pleasant garden cafe, soon turning right along a path between bushes. Cross a footbridge and turn right through a kissing gate. Now follow a gravel path through three kissing gates to return to the start.

POINTS OF INTEREST:

St Mary's Church – About 40 yards along the path through the churchyard there is a large stone slab marking the grave of a family, the victims of a brutal attack. It was in May 1870 that the village blacksmith, his wife, mother, sister and three children were axed to death. The murderer – John Jones – worked for the smith and had been charged for a hammer he had broken. Jones was hanged.

Denham Place – The house was built between 1688 and 1701 for Sir Roger Hill, at a cost of £5,591 16s 9d. It was recently the subject of major refurbishment by the Sheraton Hotel group. Whilst Denham Place was being built, Sir Roger Hill lived in the 17th-century, red-brick house with Dutch gables that stands close to the church. This house (Hill House) was more recently the home of Sir John Mills, the actor.

REFRESHMENTS:

The Horse and Barge, Denham Green.
The Garden Café by Denham Lock.
There are also several possibilities in Denham, as noted in the text.

Walk 56 **BOURNE END** 5m (8km)

Maps: OS Sheets Landranger 175; Explorer 3.

A linear walk along the Thames, with two interesting short diversions.

Start: At 856865, Marlow Station.

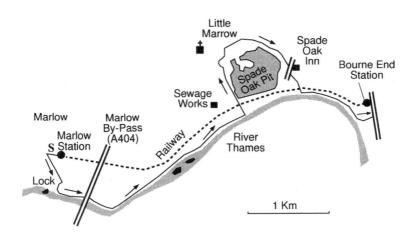

Street parking is available close to the station: please check train times for your return from Bourne End to **Marlow**. The trains run hourly on weekdays and Saturday, but less frequently on Sunday. Leave the Station at the main road and turn left along Lock Road. At the junction, turn right, ignoring a footpath on the left, to pass a number of white-fronted houses. Turn left after the Coach House, crossing a footbridge to visit Marlow Lock. To continue the walk, recross the footbridge, turn right and, after 150 yards, take the path on the right, signed as the 'Thames Path'. Follow the gravel track to join the towpath and turn left, to go under the Marlow by-pass. Continue along the towpath, passing below the wooded hillside of Winter Hill. The castle on the right has no historical origins, being a recent folly. After a mile, just beyond the sewage works and just before a kissing gate, turn left, with a hedge on your right, and go through another kissing gate. Cross the railway line, with care, go through a gate and along a path at the edge of Spade Oak Pit. Go between a pair of cottages and cross a concrete service road into Little Marlow village. A short detour is recommended here, continuing ahead to reach **Little Marlow Church** and **Manor House**.

To continue the walk, return to the stile (on the left now) almost opposite four semi-detached houses. Cross and follow a narrow path that is overgrown in summer. Cross a footbridge, walk with a wire fence on your right and cross a footbridge into a field. Turn right along the field edge, go through a wooden barrier and cross a road to the footpath opposite. Cross a gravel track, bear right to enter a small wood and continue to reach a road. Turn right, soon passing the Spade Oak Inn. Beyond a small road bridge, turn left along a gravel path signed 'Upper Thames Way'. Where the track bends left, take the right-hand path and bear right through a kissing gate to recross the railway, again with care. At the towpath T-junction, turn left and follow the path to reach the railway bridge at Bourne End. Go under the bridge, ignoring a path on the left, to arrive at a gravel area. Turn left, crossing several speed humps, then left again at the road. After 150 yards you will arrive at Bourne End Station.

POINTS OF INTEREST:

Marlow – This looks like a modern rural town, but the illusion is shattered by the fine Georgian buildings in High Street and West Street. In St Peter Street are The Old Parsonage and the Deanery, part of a 14th-century house. Marlow Place built in 1720, and the home of George II when he was Prince of Wales, is just off the High Street. The town's suspension bridge was built in 1836 by the engineer who constructed the bridge between Buda and Pest.

Little Marlow Church – The church, dedicated to St John the Baptist, dates from the 12th century, though an earlier foundation may have existed. The 12th-century tub font stands on a 19th-century stem and base. It has been used for baptisms for 800 years. During the 1980s much restoration took place, notably to the 14th-century tower and roof. A plain tombstone in the churchyard stands above the last resting place of Edgar Wallace, one of the most prolific thriller writers ever.

Little Marlow Manor House – This 16th-century house stands in 140 acres. During the 1939-45 War the Black Watch regiment occupied the house. On one occasion Queen Elizabeth, the Queen Mother, and General Eisenhower, inspected the troops and took the salute.

REFRESHMENTS:

The Spade Oak, passed on the route.

Marlow and Bourne End both have possibilities to suit every taste.

Walk 57   **LITTLE MISSENDEN**   5m (8km)

Maps: OS Sheets Landranger 165; Explorer 3.

Riverside and ancient track walking around the attractive village of Little Missenden.

Start: At 924988, in the main street between the Red Lion Inn and the Crown Inn, Little Missenden.

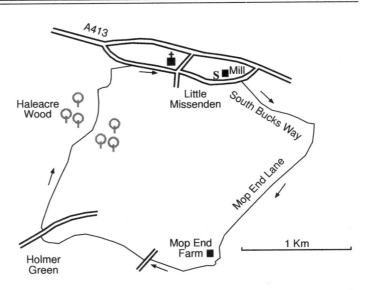

Facing either of the two inns, turn right and, ignoring a footpath directly opposite the Crown, take the path next to Toby's Farm, marked as part of the South Bucks Way. Just opposite and to the right, at the start of this path is the site of Little Missenden Mill. The rough gravel track, follows the course of the River Missbourne over to the left: where the track turns left to go over the river, cross the stile ahead and continue to another stile. Here, turn right along a track (Mop End Lane, an ancient bridleway) going uphill towards Todd's Wood. Follow the ancient lane, ignoring all turnings, for about a mile to reach its end. Go past Rose Cottage, on the left, and Mop End Farm, on the right, then bear left to continue down a tarmac lane. After 50 yards, turn right over a stile and follow a path along a field edge, walking with a hedge on your right.

At a gap in the hedge, continue ahead, keeping the hedge on your right. Go over a stile in the field corner and cross the centre of the field beyond to reach a stile on to Toby's Lane. Cross the lane and a stile and continue along the left edge of the field beyond to reach a lane. Turn left for 25 yards, then go over a stile (on the right) to the left of Beamond End Ranch. Follow a path along the right edge of a field and, where the hedge bears right, continue across the field corner, following the line of the electricity cables. Cross a stile in the corner, bear left and follow the clearly defined path into woodland, walking with a wire fence on your left. Follow the path through a fenced section, then through an area of scrub and another fenced section between gardens. On reaching a cul-de-sac turn right and, after 40 yards, at the T-junction, turn right to join a path on the left, between garages and houses. Turn right at a crossing path and, on arriving at Penfold Lane, turn right. After 30 yards, just past the 'no speed limit' signs, turn left down a signed bridleway (Kingstreet Lane).

Continue along this lane for about $^3/_4$ mile, entering Haleacre Wood. Keep to the main path through the wood, ignoring all turnings. On emerging from the wood the path continues through an alley of overhanging trees. The downhill gradient is now considerably steeper: at the bottom of the hill, ignore a path on the right and continue ahead for 100 yards. Now turn right at a crossing path, and go over a stile into a field. Follow the line of the electricity cables and, in the field corner, cross a stile on to a road. Turn right towards Little Missenden. On your way through the village you will pass **St John the Baptist's Church** and the **Manor House** before reaching the start.

POINTS OF INTEREST:

St John the Baptist's Church, Little Missenden – This is now a church of many parts, having been added to from Saxon times to the 15th century. It even incorporates some Roman bricks. The murals were rediscovered under the whitewash in 1931. The largest of these is 13th-century and shows St Christopher carrying the Child Jesus over the water, with fish around his feet. Look out, too, for the 12th-century painted wood skirting.

Manor House – The House can be seen through the wrought iron entrance gates. The part-Tudor building has been home to many whom have given loyal service to the Royal Family – notably Lady Alice Ashley and Roger Peake.

REFRESHMENTS:
The Crown Inn, Little Missenden.
The Red Lion Inn, Little Missenden.
The Bat and Ball, Holmer Green, just off the route.

Maps: OS Sheets Landranger 165; Explorer 3.
Typical Chiltern countryside north of Stokenchurch.
Start: At 761963, the Kings Arms Inn, Stokenchurch.

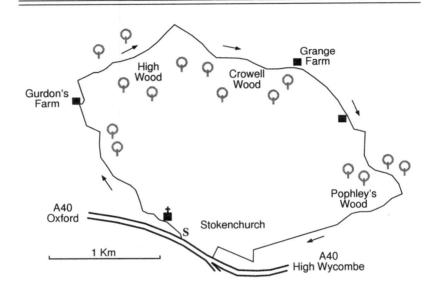

Facing the **Kings Arms**, with **Stokenchurch Church** behind, turn left and cross a minor road. Continue across a grass area with a circle of lime trees, originally the village bowling green, and, in the corner, go between Cherry Cottage and a pair of terraced cottages, to join a fenced path. Follow the path to a road and turn right. At the cul-de-sac end, turn right between houses 31 and 33. Cross a stile and follow the field edge downhill to a stile in the corner. Cross on to a path by a wire fence and follow it down to another stile. Cross, bear left and cross another stile into Stockfield Wood. To the right here there is a superb view along the valley towards High Wycombe. Take a left fork to follow the wood edge and, at the bottom, turn left and cross a stile. Go along the left edge of the field beyond, then turn right at an intermittent line of bushes. On reaching Gurdon's Farm, go through a kissing gate, bear left across a yard and go over a stile. Keep to the right field edge and cross a stile in the corner. Turn right along a track and, where the track meets level ground, turn left. Now take the right fork along a path going uphill into High Wood. On emerging at a large field, maintain direction, keeping well to the right of some storage barns. At the wood edge there is a merging of footpaths: turn left, go 10 yards past the tree with the waymarker arrows and then turn right along path CH 37. You may find the paths confusing here, but the basic direction is along the wood edge, soon with rising fields to your left. The bridleway can be very muddy, so it may be advisable to take one of the drier parallel footpaths. The 'official' route is marked with white arrows.

On reaching Grange Farm, bear left, following the white arrows to join a farm track. Follow this track, passing the farm drive and continuing along a metalled section. Pass a farm on the right, then turn left at the T-junction and, after 150 yards, turn right along a bridleway. (The village in front of you is Bennett End, where refreshment is available at the Three Horseshoes Inn). The bridleway climbs quite steeply through Pophley's Wood to arrive at the house (Pophley's). Continue ahead, down the drive, and, where it bends left, cross a stile on the right and go through a short avenue of trees. Cross a stile and the centre of the field beyond, bearing right at a hedge corner to remain on the grass track. After $^3/_4$ mile, continue ahead at a crossing path to join a narrow fenced path. The path skirts a playing field and then runs beside some modern houses: go through a metal kissing gate and continue to reach a road. Turn left and, on reaching the main road, turn right to return to the start.

POINTS OF INTEREST:

Kings Arms – Originally a 18th-century coaching inn, but given a 20th-century face lift and now undergoing further refurbishment, both externally and internally.

Stokenchurch Church – The Church of St Peter and St Paul, hidden behind the Kings Arms, is mainly 13th-century. The Norman tower supports a green copper bellcot which was added in 1893, as was the north aisle. The 15th-century brasses of two knights, both named Robert Morle, can be seen in the chancel. The church is the burial place of Hannah Ball, a friend of John Wesley, who founded the first English Sunday School in High Wycombe in 1769.

REFRESHMENTS:

The Three Horseshoes, Bennett End, just off the route.
There are several possibilities in Stokenchurch.

Walk 59   **COOMBE HILL**   5m (8km)

Maps: OS Sheets Landranger 165; Explorer 2.

A little stamina is required for this walk to the top of Coombe Hill.

Start: At 847072, the lay-by opposite the entrance to Ellesborough Golf Club.

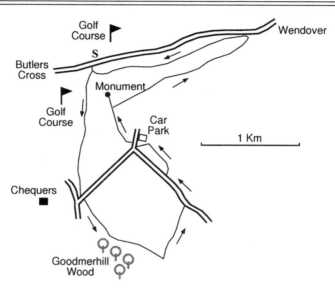

Facing the clubhouse, turn left along the road and then left along a track. Bear right through a gate by the National Trust's sign for **Coombe Hill**, then take a right fork to go uphill beside the golf course. The Coombe Hill Monument can be seen on the left. Go through a swing gate and continue ahead, go straight on at a crossing path to reach a road. The gate house opposite is part of the Chequers Estate, **Chequers** can be seen beyond the metal gate. Turn left along the road (signed for Dunsmore), then go through the horse barrier on the right, taking the centre of the paths ahead, not those on the left which go uphill. The path (a bridleway) is clearly waymarked with blue arrows. Follow the path as it climbs, ignoring a path to the right and the first Ridgeway signpost. At the second signpost, continue ahead still, following the blue arrows into the heart of

114

Goodmerhill Wood. At a crossing path, turn left, following the yellow waymarkers uphill. Near the top, cross a stile in a wire fence on the right and turn left. Go through a new plantation, cross a stile and continue ahead to cross a stile by a horse jump. Keep left of more jumps, going downhill to reach a road.

Turn left, ignoring the stile opposite and, later, the stile on the right. Follow the road uphill and, after passing 'The Lodge', turn right through a horse barrier. Bear left at the next fork, continuing along the main path. Ignore all turnings then, at the next major fork, bear left through ferns, soon bearing left again to reach a Nature Trail car park. Go through the gate in the left corner and follow the broad path beyond. Go through a gap in the trees and bear right towards the **Coombe Hill Monument**. With your back to the monument, facing the directional tablet, turn right and follow the Ridgeway markers, going through a kissing gate and crossing a sunken bridleway. Continue along the Ridgeway to the next wooded area. Now pass two wooden posts and bear left. Beyond this steeper section, go through a kissing gate on to a grassy path. Bear left at the next fork, then left again at a wooden bench. Go through a gate and, at the bottom, turn sharply left, by the Bacombe Hill notice board. You now follow this path for almost a mile. When you leave the wood, cross several stiles and follow a drive in front of some houses to reach a stile by a wooden gate. Cross to join the drive of Coombe House and turn sharp left up a path between houses – look for a yellow arrow on a beech tree. At the top, cross a stile and turn right along a sunken bridleway, going downhill to reach a road. Turn right to regain the start.

POINTS OF INTEREST:

Coombe Hill – Coombe Hill, a total of 106 acres, was presented to the National Trust in 1918 by Lord Lee of Fareham. At 832 feet (260m) the hill is almost the highest point of the Chilterns.

Chequers – Since 1922, this has been the Prime Minister's country home. It was given to the nation in 1921 by Lord Lee of Fareham. The original house was built in 1565, but altered and enlarged in the 18th and 19th centuries.

Coombe Hill Monument – The monument was raised in 1904 to honour the 148 men of Buckinghamshire who died in the Boer War. The monument is located at one of the best viewing points on the Chiltern Scarp. It was almost totally destroyed by lightning in 1938, but rebuilt in the same year by the County Council.

REFRESHMENTS:

There are none on the route, many possibilities in Wendover, a short distance eastwards. Alternatively, the Russell Arms at Butlers Cross is about 500 yards left on the main road towards Princes Risborough.

Walk 60   **WOOBURN GREEN**   5m (8km)

Maps: OS Sheets Landranger 175; Explorer 3.

A scenic walk with views over the Wye valley. The gravel workings may create some footpath diversions.

Start: At 922893, the Holtspur Hill picnic car park.

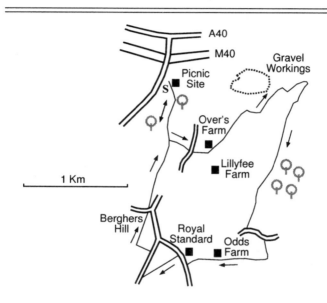

Take the path at the northern end of the car park, going through a kissing gate and turning right along a fenced path. After 80 yards, go through a kissing gate, then cross a stile and head for the corner of a wood. Cross a stile into the wood, following the well-defined path beyond. At the first crossing path, turn left, over a stile, keeping to the left of a clump of trees. Cross a stile to the left of a brick house on to a road. Cross and walk down Lillyfee Farm Lane. Where the lane bends right, turn left, under the horse barrier, on to the drive to Overs Farm. Go to the right of the farm and continue along a path between intermittent hedges. On reaching a more open area continue ahead, soon with hedges on either side. Go through a gap, keeping to the left edge of the field beyond and then turn right to walk with a wire fence on the right. Follow the fence around and, where the path meets the gravel pit, continue for another 20 yards, then turn left, keeping a line of oak trees on your left. Continue along the path to reach a footpath marker. There, turn left through a gap in the hedge. Turn right at a wire fence and left at the fence corner, with the gravel pits on your left. Turn right in the corner and, on reaching a grassy bank, turn right down a recently made track, with the bank on your left. At the end of the bank, turn left and then right along a path through the small wood. (At the time of writing, trees blocked the entrance to this path so a short diversion may be necessary.)

Leave the wood over a stile and turn left into a field with a single oak tree. Keep to the left edge, going through a gap and continuing along the side of the wood. At a fork, bear left along a wide, grassy track, across the wood corner. Cross a stile and follow the left edge to cross another stile on to a lane. Turn left and walk around a right-hand bend. Now, at a left-hand bend, continue ahead over a stile and go along the right edge of a field. In the corner, cross a stile on the right, keeping to the right edge of the next field. Cross a pair of stiles and go through a portable home site. Go past the entrance to **Odds Farm Park** and continue to reach a road. Turn right and, opposite the Royal Standard Inn, turn left through a horse barrier into the woods. Ignore a turn on the left near some dilapidated buildings and continue ahead, following the path to the right. Turn right on leaving the wood and, after 200 yards, turn left down **Berghers Hill** to reach a road. Turn right and follow the road through an area of older properties, continuing along a narrow fenced path to reach a road junction. Cross the green triangle and follow the path opposite into Mill Wood. Keep to the main bridleway through the wood, ignoring all side paths. Cross a stile to leave the wood and go across the corner of a field. Now cross a stile and go through two kissing gates to return to the start.

POINTS OF INTEREST:

Odds Farm Park – This park of rare and interesting farm breeds has been created with children in mind. There are many opportunities to observe the animals closely and safely, and to make comparisons between old and new breeds. There is also a craft shop, a log play area and tea rooms. The park is open daily from April to October. **Berghers Hill** – This very ancient part of the Wooburn parish was once known as Beggars Hill.

REFRESHMENTS:

The Royal Standard Inn, Berghers Hill.
There is a tearoom at Odds Farm Park.

Walks 61 & 62   STONE   5m (8km)
                                              or 7m (11km)

Maps: OS Sheets Landranger 165; Explorer 2.
*An easy walk to Hartwell House and, on the longer version,
Eythrope Park.*
Start: At 784123, by the church in Stone.

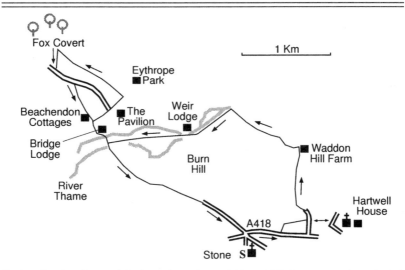

Facing the church, turn left along the main road (the A418). Ignore a path on the left
and turn left along a tarmac path before the Waggon and Horses Inn. Go through a
gate and along a drive, bear right to pass a thatched cottage. Go through a gate and
along a fenced path to a lane. Turn right and, after 100 yards, go left over a stile in the
hedge. Bear left where a path joins from the right, to follow the line of a stone wall.
To visit **Hartwell Church** and **Hartwell House** turn left, and then immediately right
through a kissing gate into the churchyard. Go past the church and continue along the
path to the House. Retrace your steps and turn right along the lane. Go past an elaborate
shelter and, after 100 yards, turn left over a stile. Cross the centre of a field and a stile,
and bear left, keeping to the left edge of a wood. Soon leave the wood, going through
a gap between stone walls. Cross a stile and turn right along a lane. Follow the lane to
a metal stile, following the left edge of the field beyond. Bear right at a marker post to

reach a stile. Now head for Waddon Hill Farm and, on reaching the barns, turn left into a field. Go through two gaps, maintaining direction across a field corner. Go ahead at the hedge corner, then through a sliding metal stile. On reaching the River Thame, turn left through a gate and follow the river. Cross stiles and a footbridge, continuing to pass, on the left, the earthworks of Burn Hill. Go through a kissing gate and, soon, cross a footbridge in front of Weir Lodge. Go along a fenced path to join a concrete track. Bear left to go beneath the chestnut trees to reach a T-junction.

The short walk turns left here, following a tarmac track (Swans Way) for about $1^1/_2$ miles to reach a crossroads opposite Stone Church.

The longer walk turns right. Go over a bridge, passing Bridge Lodge on the left. Bear right through gates and go along a tarmac track. On reaching Beachendon Cottages, turn right, still on the track. Go over a crossing track, passing The Pavilion on the right. At the gates to **Eythrope House**, turn left through a gate and go through the trees. Go through a gate to maintain direction and, on reaching a crossing path, by some wooden gates, turn sharp left, leaving Swans Way. At a tarmac track, turn left and, after 200 yards, turn right over a stile. Bear left, keeping the trees to your right. Cross a stile, continuing through a new plantation and follow the path down to Beachendon Cottages, following the track ahead. Now retrace your steps to rejoin the short walk, following it back to Stone.

POINTS OF INTEREST:

Hartwell Church – The present church, which replaced a medieval structure, was erected in 1754 for Sir William Lee of Hartwell House. After the 1939-45 War, roof lead was stolen, causing substantial damage to the building's fabric. The remains were declared redundant in 1973, though extensive work has been carried out since.

Hartwell House – The original house was built in the 1600s by Sir Thomas Lee and modernised in 1755 by the fourth baronet, Sir William Lee, who also built a church in the grounds. The grounds were laid out by Capability Brown. In 1807 the house was occupied by the exiled Louis XVIII. Unfortunately the house was internally changed without thought of conservation. In 1957 it was the home of the House of Citizenship, an organisation for the training of girls in international business affairs. It was later converted to a hotel.

Eythrope House – Built in 1883 and occupied by Alice, the sister of Ferdinand Rothschild, the builder of Waddesdon Manor.

REFRESHMENTS:
The Waggon and Horses, Stone.
The Century Arms, Stone.

Walk 63   **MUCH HADHAM**   5m (8km)

Maps: OS Sheets Landranger 167; Pathfinder 1097.

A varied walk among thatched cottages and fine houses.

Start: At 430197, St Andrew's Church, Much Hadham.

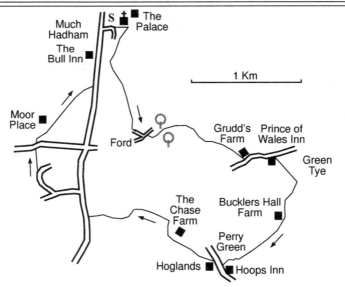

Facing the church, turn right, passing Glebe Cottage. Ignore a path and footbridge on the left and, at the right-hand bend, cross a stile. Ignore the swing gate ahead and turn left along a fenced path. Go over a footbridge, bearing right across a paddock to its top left corner. Go through a kissing gate and cross a track to a gate. Follow the left edge beyond, soon joining a stream on the right. Go through a gate, bear right away from the buildings and cross a ladder stile by a ford. Turn left along a lane and, at a T-junction, turn left to continue along the lane. After 50 yards, turn right through a gap, go over a footbridge and a stile, and turn left across a field to the stile in the corner. Follow a path through a wood and, on leaving, follow an uphill path towards a large oak. Maintain direction across a field, turning left at the half-way point and, soon, right at a T-junction. At a junction of paths, bear left into a wood corner, following a bridleway with a fence on the right. At a road by Grudd's Farm, turn left into Green Tye. Go past the greenhouses and, just after the Prince of Wales Inn, turn right along a track. Where the track goes right, go ahead along a path to a T-junction. Turn right along the right field edge. At a fork, go ahead and, in the corner, turn left along a path, passing Bucklers Hall Farm. At a T-junction, ignore a bridleway to the left, turning right along a path beside the farm boundary. Bear left along a track and, at the next marker post, follow the arrow to the right. Go along a field edge, leaving through a gap in the corner on to a road. To the left is the Hoops Inn. Cross to a footpath, keeping right of **Hoglands**. Where the tracks goes left, cross a stile and bear right along a field edge. Pass Chase Farm, and, on reaching a line of intermittent trees, turn right along a grass track. After 200 yards, turn left towards Sidehill Wood. At the wood, turn left, then right at the wood corner, following a path downhill. Cross a stile and footbridge and go past a pumping station to reach a road. Turn right, then left along Station Road. Turn right at the T-junction and, on the right-hand bend, turn left along a track by some rear gardens. Cross a stile on to a road. Go up the steps, through a gate, cross a gravel area and bear right, Moor Place is on the left. Cross a stile by a metal gate and keep right of the farm buildings to a stile in a fence. Bear right to a stile by the tennis courts and turn right along a track to a road. Turn left along **Much Hadham** High Street, passing some very attractive properties, including the Bull Inn. At the end of the High Street turn right to return to the church.

POINTS OF INTEREST:

Hoglands – This was the home and workplace of the sculptor Henry Moore from 1940 until his death in 1986. He is buried at St Thomas' Church, Perry Green. The Henry Moore Foundation now manages the site. Open days are regularly held at the Foundation and some examples of Moore's work can be seen from the walk.

Much Hadham – The village, one of Hertfordshire's oldest and certainly most interesting villages, as Saxon origins. The High Street has many historic buildings including the Forge Museum, with a working forge, a Victorian cottage and a unique 19th-century bee house. The Hall was built in 1726 and was, until recently, the home of the poet Walter de la Mare's son. The Bull Inn was built in about 1727. St Andrew's Church is set in a beautiful churchyard. It has two Henry Moore works, the heads of a King and Queen. The oldest item is a door which hangs in the priest's vestry. It has hinge straps and dates from 1225. The Palace, behind the church is 16th-century and was a bishop's palace, a school and an asylum before conversion for residential use.

REFRESHMENTS:
The Prince of WalesInn, Green Tye.
The Hoops Inn, Perry Green.
The Bull Inn, Much Hadham.

Walk 64   **THORNBOROUGH**   5m (8km)

Maps: OS Sheets Landranger 165 and 152; Pathfinder 1046.

*A pretty walk along the River Ouse and a disused canal, passing
many sites of archaeological and historical interest.*

Start: At 745336, the Two Brewers Inn, Thornborough.

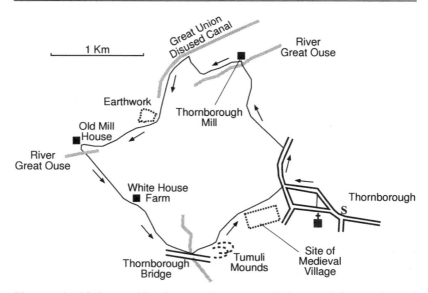

Please park with due consideration to residents. From the inn, turn left along the road
towards Buckingham, passing the Wesleyan Chapel, the old village pump and
St Mary's Church. About 50 yards beyond the village school, turn right to go through
a small paddock. Cross a footbridge and a stile, and bear left across another footbridge.
Go through a gate to reach a road and turn left. At the T-junction, turn right and, after
200 yards, ignore a path on the left, continuing for another 200 yards and then turning
left along a concrete track. Where the track bears left, go right to follow a wide grass
path. Bear right at a marker post, then left at the hedge corner, continuing with the
hedge on your right. In the corner, go over a stile and bear left of the single-storey
building to cross another stile. Turn left over a stream, with Thornborough Mill (now
converted to residential units) on the right.

Go through a gravel area, turn left and then right over the footbridge crossing a weir. Bear left to cross a stile, following the line of the river beyond to cross another stile. Bear right through a small paddock (very overgrown in summer), then cross three footbridges to enter a wooded area. Turn left along the towpath of the now disused **Buckingham Arm** of the Grand Union Canal. Go over a ladder stile and continue ahead. After passing a pumping station, the outline of an Iron Age earthworks can be seen on the right. Cross a stile, following a wire fence to go through a gate, and continue across a narrow field. Cross a stile on to a lane, with the Old Mill House on the right. Turn left, crossing the river, then leave the lane, bearing left to cross a double stile. Bear right to reach a stile just left of the corner. Cross and head just to the right of White House Farm, crossing a stile in a fence and maintaining direction to cross a stile in the corner. Go over another stile and bear left to cross a stile by a gate. Go over a farm track and bear right, keeping to the left of a (usually dried up) pond to reach a stile. Cross and bear right, downhill, into the field corner. Turn right over a stile and left along a track to cross **Thornborough Bridge**. Now, before the car park, turn left over a stile, then bear right, keeping left of the **Thornborough Mounds**.

After passing the mounds, bear left to cross a stile 50 yards to the right of the top left-hand corner. Turn left along a tarmac path and, after 80 yards, turn right along the drive of Western Green Farm. Bear left at the farm gates to go through a metal gate. There are great views from here, both in front and behind. Bear right as you cross the site of a medieval village, then cross a ladder stile and bear left to go through two gates on to a lane. Follow the lane to a road and turn right over a bridge. At the T-junction, turn left to return to Thornborough village centre.

POINTS OF INTEREST:

Buckingham Arm – The canal opened in 1801 mainly to carry coal, but trade had declined by 1910 with the success of the railways. It was finally abandoned in 1961 and is now a nature reserve.

Thornborough Bridge – This, the only surviving medieval bridge in Buckinghamshire, dating from the 14th century. The road was routed over a new bridge in 1974 to ensure its survival.

Thornborough Mounds – The two obvious burial mounds are of Roman origin, probably 2nd-centuryAD. Excavations in 1840 found many items such as bronze lamps and pottery. These are now housed in the Cambridge University Museum.

REFRESHMENTS:

The Two Brewers Inn, Thornborough.
The Lone Tree Inn, about $^1/_2$ mile east of Thornborough Bridge.

Walk 65   **BAYFORD**   5m (8km)

Maps: OS Sheets Landranger 166; Pathfinder 1120.

Fine houses, pretty cottages, pleasant paths and two lovely inns.

Start: At 311083, the car park opposite the Bakers Arms, Bayford.

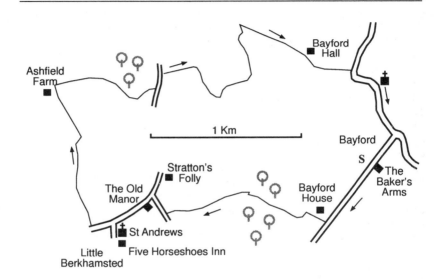

Facing the Bakers Arms, turn right along the road, passing the Memorial Hall, primary school and Bayford Grange on the right. Pass the drive to Bayford House and, after 30 yards, turn right along a gravel track. Bear left at a gate on to a narrow path. Cross a stile and go along the right edge of a field. Turn right at a hedge corner, walking along the field's right boundary. Cross a stile into Bayford Wood. Go over a crossing track and continue downhill to a footpath marker post. Bear right, then left, continuing downhill. Go over a footbridge and bear left along a path signed for Little Berkhamsted. To the right is **Stratton's Folly**. Cross three stiles and keep left of a metal gate, going along a narrow fenced path. Cross a stile and turn right along a lane. Ignore a stile on the left, continuing past the Old Manor to reach a T-junction. Turn left, passing St Andrew's Church and the War Memorial. To the left is the Five Horseshoes Inn. Continue ahead and, after 100 yards, turn right through a gate and go long a gravel drive. Continue through a grassy area, then go through a gate and follow the left edge through another gate. Continue along a path at the left edge and, in the corner, go through a gate to join a path signed for Howe Green. On reaching Ashfield Farm, on the left, turn right and cross a stile and the centre of the next field. Keep just to the right of a single oak, then bear right, heading for the house visible in the trees. Go through a gap and along a rough track. Bear right, following the track to skirt Culver Wood and reach a road. Turn left and, after 150 yards, turn right through a gate, signed for Bayford. Leave the tarmac track after 100 yards, continuing with a hedge on your right. Cross a stile, go along a narrow fenced path and cross a stile on to a tarmac track. Bear right in front of 'Little Stockings', following the track past a bungalow (Swallow Mead). Turn left on a path signed for Waterhall. On reaching 'Great Stockings', bear left, keeping the house on your left, to follow a bridleway. The sunken stretch of this bridleway is muddy whatever the time of the year. Go over a footbridge on the edge of a wood and bear left, following the bridleway and ignoring a path on the right. After 60 yards, at a marker post, turn right, uphill, into the centre of the wood. Keep to the main path, continuing uphill. The path is reasonably easy to see on the ground, but goes through an area of overhanging bushes. Leave the wood, heading for the house in the distance. Bayford Hall is on the left, beyond the trees. After a horse jump, on the left, follow a path along the edge of the wood. In the corner, go along a narrow, fenced path to reach a road. Turn right following the road uphill towards St Mary's Church, Bayford. Continue along the road back to **Bayford**, turn righting at the T-junction to return to the Bakers Arms.

POINTS OF INTEREST:

Stratton's Folly – Also known as Admiral's Folly. Retired Admiral John Stratton decided to build a tower so that he could see ships sailing up the Thames. The 100ft red-brick tower was built in 1789 and is now a private residence.

Bayford – The village's oldest houses are found on the road to Epping Green. Two of these are passed on the walk, Bayford Grange and Bayford House, the latter having some superb outbuildings. The Baker family has always been a great benefactor of the village, replacing the old parish church, providing a village school and presenting the village with a Memorial Hall in 1913. In the village churchyard lies William Yarrell, born 1784, whose books on British birds and fishes were considered the best on the subjects of their time.

REFRESHMENTS:
The Bakers Arms, Bayford.
The Five Horseshoes Inn, Little Berkhamsted.

Walk 66   ESSENDON   5m (8km)

Maps: OS Sheets Landranger 166; Pathfinder 1120.
Along the banks of the River Lea.
Start: At 273088, St Mary's Church, Essendon.

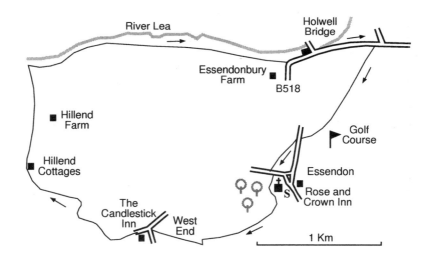

Facing **St Mary's Church** gate, turn right at the T-junction, and then turn left, passing the now closed, Salisbury Crest Inn. Turn left after the old inn, following a fenced path. Go through a kissing gate and bear right across a paddock. Cross two stiles and continue along the left field edge. Cross a stile and bear right to cross another by a small pond, entering Backhouse Wood. Turn right, keeping initially to the wood edge. Ignore a path to the right and cross a stile into a less densely wooded area, going downhill. Go over a footbridge and through a hedge gap, keeping to the right edge of the field beyond. At a T-junction, turn left along a rough track and, after 10 yards, turn right along a path through the trees. After 30 yards, turn left through a gap, then turn right along the field edge. In the corner, cross a stile and follow a fenced path to a stile on to a lane by the Candlestick Inn, in West End.

Cross the lane and continue ahead along a minor lane signed as a 'No Through Road'. Go past Flint Cottage and a group of cottages, then turn right after the next single cottage to go along a gravel track. Follow this winding track to reach Hillend Cottages. Continue along a tarmac track, passing Hillend Farm on the right. On reaching the River Lea, turn right along a well-defined path, with the river on your left. Ignore a path and footbridge on the left, and a track to the right, maintaining direction for $1\frac{1}{2}$ miles, passing Essendonbury Farm on the right and keeping to the left of a small gravel pit, to reach a road.

Turn right, then bear left along the main road (the B158), following it with care and soon passing Essendon Mill, on the left. Go past Holwell Lane and Holwell Bridge, on the left. There is a 600 yard stretch of road walking here, without a footpath, so do exercise extreme caution on this sometimes busy road.

Before the next turning on the left, go over a stile on the right to reach a golf course. Keep to the tarmac track, heading for the church. On reaching a footpath marker post, turn right along a gravel track. At the next T-junction, turn right and, after 20 yards, turn left along a narrow path between hedges. Cross a stile, keeping to the right of the Parsonage, to reach a lane. Cross the lane and follow the footpath opposite, bearing left across a field. The stile you want is just to the right of the last house. Cross on to a lane and turn left to return to Essendon and the church.

POINTS OF INTEREST:

St Mary's Church, Essendon – The tower dates from the 15th century, but the bulk of the building was restored in 1883. The interior contains a rare black Wedgewood font from 1778, given to the church by Mary Whitbread. In the graveyard is the tomb of the Rev Richard Orme who died in 1843. He was so worried about being buried alive that the tomb was built above ground with a door. He was buried with a key to the door, a bottle of wine and a loaf of bread. A plaque on the south-facing wall commemorates the re-building of the church after it was bombed by a German Zeppelin in 1916. The Zeppelin was brought down 4 miles away in the village of Cuffley.

Essendon – Some of the houses near the church display the Salisbury crest, confirming the links with the Salisbury family who lived at nearby Hatfield House. Many splendid houses can be seen in the area, particularly to the south of the village. Bedwell Park, once the home of the Whitbreads (the brewers), is now a country club. Camfield Place, visited by Beatrix Potter as a child, is now the home of Barbara Cartland.

REFRESHMENTS:
The Rose and Crown, Essendon.
The Candlestick Inn, West End.

Walk 67   **STEWKLEY**   5m (8km)

Maps: OS Sheets Landranger 165; Pathfinder 1071.

Peace and solitude to the west of Stewkley.

Start: At 852262 opposite the Post Office, High Street, Stewkley.

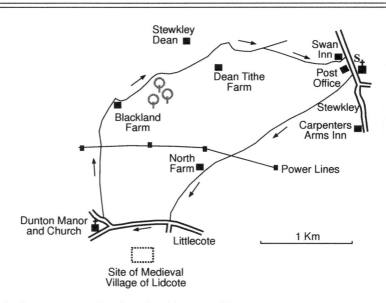

Take the concrete track to the right of the Post Office, crossing a stile to an overgrown path along the rear of houses. Go through a more open area, following the hedge on the right. Cross a stile and footbridge in the corner to reach another stile. Continue with a hedge on your left then, in the corner, go through a gap and continue, now with the hedge on your right. Cross a stile and footbridge, and continue to cross a pair of stiles in the corner. Turn left over a stile and go along the left field edge, with North Farm ahead. Go through a gate, turn right and, immediately, left through a gate. Bear left across a field, cross a stile in the top left corner and bear left to a track. Turn left along the track to reach a road in Littlecote. Turn right and, as you pass Knapps Farm, on the right, the site of the medieval village of **Lidcote** is on both sides of the road. At the road junction, ignore a path on the right and go up the lane signed for Hoggeston. After 200 yards, turn right at a gate and go along the left field edge. Go over an awkward double stile, maintaining direction to go through a gate below a pylon. Now head for the water tower at Mursley. Go through a gate and turn right along the field edge. After the hedge corner, turn right over a pair of stiles. Cross a gravel area in front of Blackland Farm, go through two gates and bear left across a paddock to join a gravel track. Go through a gap in a hedge, then, where the track bears left, go ahead across a field. Go over a cattle grid and turn right to a gate. Turn left over a footbridge and stile to the right of an oak tree. Cross a double stile in a hedge and continue over two more stiles, with Stewkley Dean on the left. In the corner, go ahead, under the telephone lines, passing Dean Tithe Farm on the right. Go over a stile, turn right along a concrete track and, after 15 yards, turn left over a stile. In the right field corner, turn right over a stile and, after 20 yards, cross a stile on the left. Bear right across a field to go over a double stile in the corner. After 15 yards, turn left over a double stile and, before reaching an oak tree in the corner, turn right over a double stile and bear left across a field, heading for the tower of Stewkley church. In the left corner, go through a gate, then cross a stile to the right of a pond. Skirt the pond and turn right over a footbridge and stile. Bear left, still heading for the church, to cross a stile in a fence. Cross a stile in the right-hand hedge and bear left to the corner of a bungalow. Cross a stile and turn left along a concrete track to reach the Swan Inn. Turn right to reach **St Michael's Church** and the start.

POINTS OF INTEREST:

Stewkley – The village has one of the longest High Streets in England, over $1^1/_2$ miles. No 14 Ivy lane, a 16th-century cottage, was once the home of Mrs. Pankhurst and her daughter Sylvia, the leaders of the 'votes for women' campaign.

Lidcote – This important medieval earthworks site was threatened by farming expansion in 1992, but thankfully remains intact. On either side of the road a series of house platforms can be seen and there is documentary evidence of a manor house and chapel. The old village was enclosed in 1494 and totally destroyed in 1517.

St Michael's Church, Stewkley – This beautiful and unspoilt Norman church dates from 1120. With its squat tower and recessed west door, it is one of the finest Norman buildings in the country. Over 6,000 churches were built by the Normans, but only three have survived without major later additions to their original plan. It is said that Oliver Cromwell and his soldiers put their horses in the church when artillery was brought to Pitch Hill Green.

REFRESHMENTS:

The Swan, High Street, Stewkley.
The Carpenters Arms, at the southern end of Stewkley.

STOKE HAMMOND

Maps: OS Sheets Landranger 165; Pathfinder 1071.
Climbing Partridge Hill to the west of Stoke Hammond.
Start: At 881295, the Post Office, Stoke Hammond.

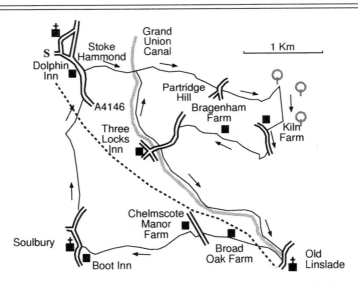

Rejoin the main road and turn left down Bragenhamside, opposite the Dolphin Inn.
Pass a school and go along a tarmac track. Go over a canal bridge (reached later by
the shorter walk) and through a white gate, passing Paper Mill Farm, to cross the
bridge over the River Ouzel. Now follow a track, ignoring a bridleway on the left. Go
through a gate and up Partridge Hill to reach a road. Turn right, and immediately left
along a bridleway, soon entering Oak Wood. At a crossing path, turn right along the
signed Greensand Ridge Walk. Bear right over a stile and follow the woodland edge.
Beyond Kiln Farm, on the right, the path has been diverted: continue for 200 yards,
then cross a new stile on the right and bear left across a field to reach a stile on to a
road. Cross to a track and, after 150 yards, just before Ludley Cottage, bear right.
Bear right through scrub and cross a footbridge and a stile. Turn left over a footbridge
and cross a field. Go through ferns and cross a stile. Go past a series of ponds and

cross a track, keeping a fence on your left. Cross two stiles and bear left, with Bragenham Farm on your right. Cross a stile and a field to reach a stile into a wood (the ground is always wet here). Bear left to leave the wood, going over a crossing track and skirting the farm garden. Cross a stile to reach a fence corner. The next marker is on a telegraph post: go through trees, cross a stile and bear left through a gate. Cross a stile in the bottom corner and bear left to a stile on to a road. Go left, crossing the Red Bridge and, at a left-hand bend, go ahead to the **Three Locks** Inn.

The shorter walk crosses the bridge to join the canal towpath, following it northwards to reach the footbridge crossed earlier. From here, reverse the outward journey to the start.

The longer walk does not cross the bridge: instead, turn left along the towpath, following it for about $1^1/_2$ miles. Leave the canal at the bridge by **Old Linslade**. Cross the bridge and, after 100 yards, turn right, then bear left and cross a railway footbridge. Bear right, heading to the left of Broad Oak Farm. Go through a gap and continue to cross a stile and track. Go past a large oak, continuing across the centre of a field. Cross two stiles on to a road. Turn left, and immediately right to cross a stile. Go through a small wood, cross a stile and turn right, then left, before the first barn, to go along a wide track. Go through a gap and bear left across a field corner to a gap. Bear right and cross four stiles and footbridges, heading towards the tower of Soulbury Church. Bear left (into the top corner) to a stile and follow a wide track through a kissing gate to join a gravel track. Follow this to a road opposite the church. The Boot Inn is to the left. Turn right, ignoring Chapel Hill on the right and, at the fork by the Forge, bear right towards Stoke Hammond. At the top of the green, by the thatched cottage, go ahead along a signed track, following it for 1,000 yards. After a left bend, at a crossing track, turn right and go under the railway to reach a road. Turn left to return to the start.

POINTS OF INTEREST:

Three Locks – The three locks were built in 1800 to lower the narrow boats by 6 metres on their journey north.

Old Linslade – Not much remains of the old village, except the Manor House and the original parish church. The Manor is a fine 18th-century red and grey brick house. St Mary's Church was built in the 12th century of limestone and iron stone. It transferred its functions to the larger St Barnabas' Church in Linslade new town.

REFRESHMENTS:

The Dolphin Inn, Stoke Hammond.
The Boot Inn, Soulbury.

Maps: OS Sheets Landranger 165; Pathfinder 1070.
Field paths around the Claydons.
Start: At 740256, East Claydon Church.

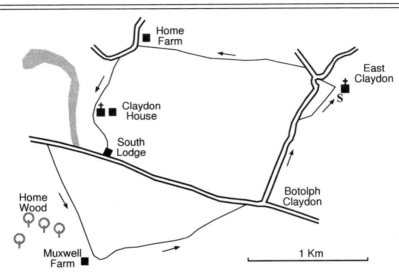

Return to the main road and turn left. After 50 yards, turn right along a road signed for
Steeple Claydon. Go past a wooden-framed, thatched cottage dated 1641 and, after
Verney Farm, on the left, turn left through a metal gate, going diagonally across a
field. Keep left of a metal gate to go through a wooden gate. Follow the right field
edge, go through a gate and maintain direction across a field, soon continuing along a
wire fence with intermittent bushes on the left. Go past a small pond, cross a stile in
the corner and follow the left field edge, going through a gap in the corner and heading
for the barns of Home Farm. At the lane, turn left, passing a small cemetery, then,
80 yards beyond a telephone box, turn left along a path beside a converted house.
Bear right across a field towards **Claydon House**. Go through a gate on the right to
reach the drive and turn right through a kissing gate, keeping the house to your left.
Go past Middle Claydon Church, following a wall, then bear right, leaving the wall,
to go through a gate. Follow the drive to reach a lane by South Lodge and turn right.
The area to the right, Claydon Park, is an open access area, the public being allowed

to walk the paths throughout the park and around the lake. After 600 yards, at the brow of the hill, turn left over a stile and bear left, heading for the near left corner of Home Wood. Cross a stile in an electric fence and bear left to another stile. Bear right to a stile to the right of the last electricity pole, and bear left into the top field corner. Continue ahead by a marker post and, after 10 yards, turn left through a gap. Keep Muxwell Farm on your right, cross a stile and cross a concrete area. Cross a drive, go through a metal gate, and bear left to go through a gap beneath the trees. Bear left to a stile below the oak tree in the fence opposite, and bear right into the far field corner, heading towards the thatched cottages of Botolph Claydon. Go through a gap in the corner and along the right field edge to go through a gap on to a track. Turn left, and immediately right over a footbridge and stile. Maintain direction diagonally across a field and go through a metal gate. Bear left to the field corner. Now ignore a stile on the left, and cross a stile in front of a thatched cottage. Turn left through the garden and go through a wooden gate on to a road. Turn right, then left along a road signed for East Claydon. Walk through the village of Botolph Claydon, passing the public library and the memorial to Sir Edmund Verney who gave the village the hall and library. Go past the village school and, soon, the unusual Mushroom Seat, a thatched wooden seat constructed around the base of a living oak tree. Now ignore a stile on the right, bearing right along a tarmac footpath. At a T-junction, turn left to return to **St Mary's Church, East Claydon.**

POINTS OF INTEREST:

Claydon House – Sir Ralph Verney purchased the house in 1456 and leased it to the Giffard family for 100 years. The Verneys took residence again in 1543 and have remained in occupation ever since. The house is not the original Claydon, having being rebuilt in 1750-80. The lavish decorations of the interior are hard to match in any other house in the country. Sir Harry Verney married Parthenope Nightingale, sister of the famous Florence, who visited the house a great deal and towards the end of her life settled here permanently. The house was purchased by the National Trust in 1956 and contains the bedroom and many momentoes of Florence Nightingale's life. The most notable a letter from Queen Victoria enclosing a brooch 'to commemorate your great and blessed work – which I hope you will wear as a mark of appreciation of your sovereign'.

St Mary's Church, East Claydon – Built in the 13th and 14th centuries, but restored in Victorian times by J O Scott.

REFRESHMENTS:

None on the route, but available at Steeple Claydon, Winslow and Quainton.

FURNEUX PELHAM

Maps: OS Sheets Landranger 167; Pathfinder 1074.

With excellent views across the Hertfordshire countryside, a Nature Reserve and many very pretty thatched cottages.

Start: At 432279, St Mary's Church, Furneux Pelham.

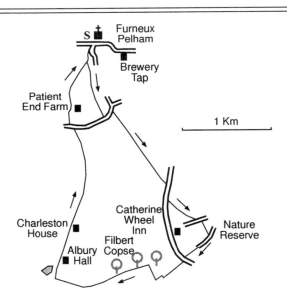

With your back to **St Mary's Church**, turn right, and immediately left down a lane. Go past the Star, until recently an inn, and head for the far left corner of the old car park to cross a footbridge. Far over to the right is **Furneux Pelham Hall**. Turn left along a path, ignoring the stile ahead, to go through a plantation. Cross a pair of stiles and go along the left edge of a field. Cross two stiles and pass Patient End Farm, on the right. Cross a stile on to a lane and turn left. Follow the lane uphill for 200 yards, then, just before a thatched cottage, turn right along a bridleway. Go over a footbridge and maintain direction towards the hedge opposite to reach a road. Turn right and, after passing a wooden bungalow, turn left along a signed path. On emerging into open country, cross the centre of a field and, in the corner, go along the side of a cottage and turn left along a gravel track. Go past some very attractive thatched cottages and follow the track to reach a lane. Cross and continue ahead, cross the Patmore Heath Nature Reserve. Go over a crossing track to reach a road and turn right. Where the road bends right, go ahead, in front of a wooden cottage, to reach a fenced path, following it to reach a road. (Turn right here to reach the Catherine Wheel Inn, Gravesend. The walk turns left. Now, before the farm buildings, turn right along a gravel bridleway. Go over a bridge and follow the wide track to the corner of a narrow wood (Filbert Copse). Turn left, keeping the copse on your right. In the corner, continue ahead, with the wood now on your left. In the next corner join a tarmac drive and turn right, following it to the end of the wood. Turn right through a kissing gate and follow a path along the wood edge. Take care not to miss this path, as it is often overgrown. Go past a large pond, on the left, and emerge to cross two stiles on to a lane. Continue ahead, initially going downhill. Go past Albury House, behind the trees to the right.

Where the track bears left, continue ahead with Charleston House on the right. At the corner by the pond, turn right, and then immediately left along a path running parallel with the hedge. Follow the path as it bears left, downhill, to cross a footbridge. Continue ahead along a wide grass path to reach a road. Turn left, and, after 30 yards, turn right up the drive to Patient End Farm. Pass the farm on the right and, at a fork, turn right, passing the brick buildings to go over a stile by a metal gate. Keep to the left edge of a field to reach a stile, and bear slightly right to a stile at the end of the tree line. Bear right into a field corner, cross two stiles and go through a small wood returning to the car park of the old Star Inn. Turn left to return to the church.

POINTS OF INTEREST:

St Mary's Church, Furneux Pelham – The chancel dates from the 13th century, but the embattled tower with its Hertfordshire spike and gargoyles, was added in 1370. A 17th-century figure of Father Time surmounts the clock. It has the cryptic inscription 'Time Flies – Mind your business'. About 850 years have passed since the Norman family of 'de Furneux' gave the village part of its name. With its many thatched cottages and listed buildings it comes as no surprise to learn that the village is often a finalist in the county's Best Kept Village competition.

Furneux Pelham Hall – The village squire still lives and farms at the Hall, which was once owned by Lord Monteagle who helped foil Guy Fawkes' Gunpowder Plot in 1605. He disclosed a letter he had received from his brother-in-law to the Privy Council at Westminster.

REFRESHMENTS:

The Brewery Tap, Furneux Pelham, on the road to Little Hadham.
The Catherine Wheel Inn, Gravesend.

Maps: OS Sheets Landranger 153 and 154; Pathfnder 1049.

An easy walk visiting three interesting villages and returning along a stretch of the Icknield Way.

Start: At 323345, All Saints' Church, Sandon.

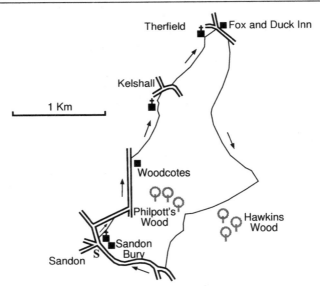

Go through the church gate and immediately turn left along a path through the churchyard, keeping the church on your right. Leave the churchyard and continue along a narrow, fenced path to reach a lane. Turn right and follow the lane around a left-hand bend to reach a T-junction (with a public byway to the right). Turn left, and, after passing the 'Woodcotes', on the right, turn right over a footbridge and follow a signed footpath. Bear left across the field, go over a crossing track and cross a stile. Cross the next field and, on reaching the fence corner, turn left and almost immediately right over a stile. Bear left to reach a wooden gate and St Faith's Church at **Kelshall**. Go through the churchyard, passing the remains of an old preaching cross, and leave along a narrow path. Turn left along a tarmac drive to reach a T-junction. Turn right and, at the green triangle, turn right along Kelshall Street. After 150 yards, turn left along a signed path, following the right edge of a field. Soon the path bears left across the centre of the field, heading for St Mary's Church at **Therfield**. Bear right, following the prominent path across the next field, ignoring a path on the left. Continue to a hedge gap and bear left. Now, in the corner, turn left to head directly for the church. Go through the gate into the churchyard and leave through a wooden gate, following a tarmac track to reach the main road opposite the Fox and Duck Inn.

Turn right along the minor road, following the waymarkers for the Icknield Way. After 200 yards, take the path, on the right, beneath an electricity cable post. Cross a stile and ignore a path to the right, continuing ahead across the centre of the field. The next stile is just to the left of the power lines, by a metal gate. Cross and continue ahead to cross another stile. Bear right across a field corner, cross a stile on the left and turn right along a gravel track. The track narrows to go through bushes. Even in dry weather this section can be very wet. Now, ignore a path to the left, continuing ahead through a wooded area, soon ignoring another path, on the right. On reaching a wider track, maintain direction ahead (signed for 'Chapel Green'). At the fork, bear left to follow a path through trees. After crossing a footbridge turn right along a signed track for Notley Green, following the track for $^3/_4$ mile, passing Hawkins Wood on the left. Ignore a footpath on the right and, on reaching the edge of Philpott's Wood, turn left, remaining on the bridleway and walking with the wood on your right, to reach a tarmac drive. Turn left to reach a road and turn right, uphill, to return to **Sandon**.

POINTS OF INTEREST:

Kelshall – The village lies approximately 550 feet up on the East Anglian Heights, a line of hills that are the beginnings of the Chilterns. St Faith's Church is unique in having every roof beam decorated with a delicately beautiful floral design. There are also painted screens of great rarity.

Therfield – St Mary's Church was built in the 13th century, but due to subsidence was rebuilt in 1874, the present church being substantially larger than its predecessor. The list of rectors inside the church goes back to before 1267.

Sandon – All Saints' Church was originally a timber-framed building, but was converted to its present form in 1348. The tower contains five bells dated between 1624 and 1728. The village has become known for its flower festival held in the church during two days each September.

REFRESHMENTS:

The Chequers Inn, Sandon.
The Fox and Duck Inn, Therfield.

Maps: OS Sheets Landranger 175; Explorer 3.
Woodland and field paths north of Beaconsfield to Hertfordshire
House, with the longer version returning through Hogback Wood.
Start: 941912, the Station or High Street car parks, Beaconsfield.

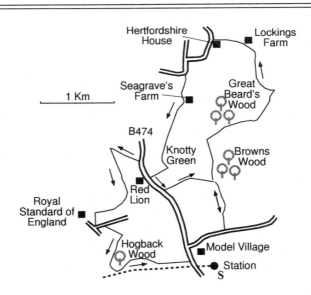

From either car park, walk along the main road, away from the station, and turn right,
down Ledborough Lane. Go past the goods entrance to **Bekonscot Model Village**
and turn left by the post box. At the fork, bear left, walking with a fence on your left.
Ignore a path on the right, bearing right into woodland at the fork. Go over a crossing
track and, at the junction markers, cross a stile on to footpath B4. Follow the path
uphill through the wood. After a pair of stiles and a gate you will emerge at Wood
Cottage: walk ahead to a lane, at the second gate, and turn left along a downhill path.
At a crossing path, at the valley bottom, turn left along a wide track. Bear right at a
fork and, after 200 yards, bear right at a white arrow on a single tree. Go uphill and
bear left near the top. In the field corner, turn right and, as the track bears right,

continue ahead along the field edge. After 10 yards, turn right through a gap and walk along the edge of the wood. In the corner, ignore a gate on the right and continue ahead, going through a gate and bearing left to reach a gate. Go through and follow a fenced track. Cross a stile and bear left, towards Hertfordshire House, to reach a lane. Turn left, following the lane around a right-hand bend to reach a T-junction. Turn left and, where the lane bends right, continue ahead along a private road. Follow this concrete track past Seagrave's Farm, then bear right in front of a storage barn on to a gravel track. Follow this track to the corner of Sandels Wood. Now, ignore a path into the wood and continue ahead, going through a gap in the corner and turning right along the field edge. Follow the path into a corner and turn right along a lane to the main road (the B474).

For the short walk, turn left and then left again into Knottocks Drive. At its end, go over the stile ahead and turn right to follow a path along the wood edge. At the end of the fence, turn right, retracing your outward steps back to the start in **Beaconsfield**.

For the longer route, turn right, passing the Red Lion Inn. Near the top of the hill, turn left at a sign for Whitchert Close. After 30 yards, bear right up a narrow path. Briefly enter a wood and, after 40 yards, turn sharp left and continue uphill to a stile. Cross this, then ignore a stile on the left and go over the stile ahead. Cross a stile, and ignore a gate to the left, bearing right to follow the fence line. Go over a series of stiles and, at the top of the hill, go over a pair of stiles and turn left over a stile on to a track, following it to a road. Turn left, then right by a telephone box and go over a stile, heading towards Hogback Wood (presented to the National Trust in 1925). Ignore stiles left and ahead, and turn right into the wood. At a fork, bear right, downhill, along the wood edge. In the corner, bear left, remaining on the level path. Bear left at the next fork and right along the next crossing path. At the railway, turn left and then bear left, keeping to the main path. Bear right at a fork, leaving the wood to join a lane. Continue ahead at the road, bearing right at a T-junction to reach the High Street.

POINTS OF INTEREST:

Bekonscot Model Village – A short diversion is required to visit the oldest model village in the world. Time has stood still in the village, with its fully working model railway, for 65 years.

Beaconsfield – The name means 'field of beeches'. GK Chesterton lived in the town between 1909 and 1935, during which time he wrote his Father Brown stories.

REFRESHMENTS;

The Red Lion, Knotty Green.

There is a varied selection in Beaconsfield.

Maps: OS Sheets Landranger 165; Pathfinder 1093.
An easy walk from Long Crendon to Shabbington.
Start: At 694085, The Square, Long Crendon.

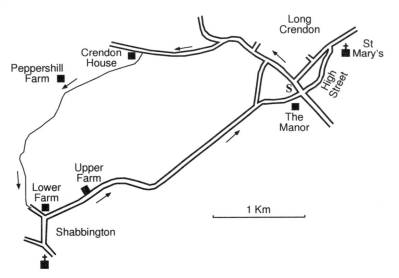

With your back to the Post Office, turn left along the main road, passing the Star Inn, and, later, both the Angel Inn and the Chandos Arms. Go past a speed de-restriction sign and, where the main road, goes downhill, bear left along a country lane. After passing Bailey's Farm, on the right, the lane bears right in front of Crendon House. Here, turn left over a stile. Turn right along the side of Crendon House, cross a stile and follow the right edge of the field beyond. Go through a gap in the corner and continue ahead. Now ignore a signed path to the left, and go through a gap, maintaining direction. Just before the corner, at the crossing path marker, with Peppershill Farm on your right, turn right and, almost immediately, left through a gap. Bear left across the corner of the field beyond, heading for a metal gate in a hedge. Go through and walk with a hedge on your right to reach some cattle barns. Here, follow the path to the left, walking with a ditch on your right and, after 30 yards, turn right into a field.

Bear slightly left away from the farm and the buildings on the right and, at the crossing path just before a tarmac road, turn left towards the village of Shabbington. Go through a metal gate in the corner and turn left along a track. Bear right through some metal gates, then pass between cottages, soon going uphill to reach a lane. Turn left along the lane, following it for about $1^1/_2$ miles towards Long Crendon. (If you would prefer to return along field paths, turn left over a stile just after leaving Shabbington and head roughly northwards to reach the crossing paths, with Peppershill Farm ahead. There, turn right to reach Crendon House and retrace your steps along the lane to Long Crendon.)

On reaching the **Long Crendon** village sign, bear right along Frogmore Lane. Near the top you will pass The Manor, on the right. Soon after you will arrive back at The Square. If you now have some spare time, stroll down the High Street to see the **St Mary's Church** and the **Court House**.

POINTS OF INTEREST:

Long Crendon – This lovely old village was once a centre for the needle making industry, manufacturing being carried on in the homes of the workers. Many of the cottages have specially made cupboards for the storing of the finished article. In some cottages the cupboards were accessible from the adjoining cottage, facilitating an easy passage between manufacturing processes.

St Mary's Church – The church dates from the 13th century, but has been substantially restored and repaired several times over the centuries. One of the features of the interior is the west window in which is incorporated the design of the west door below. South of the church there is evidence of medieval fish ponds. In contrast to St Mary's is the new Roman Catholic church, completed in 1971. It was built virtually unaided by the parish priest and three helpers working evenings and weekends over a period of 6 years.

The Court House – This was the first property obtained by the National Trust in 1900. It cost £400 with £350 being spent on restoration. Dating from the late 14th century and built of red brick, wattle and daub, the house was originally used as a wool store. It was used to hold manorial courts in the 15th century, a practice discontinued in the 1820s. It is open from April to September, on Wednesday afternoons, Sundays and Bank Holidays.

REFRESHMENTS:

There is a wide selection in Long Crendon, including those mentioned in the text.

Walk 76   **CHANDLERS CROSS**   5¹/₂m (8km)

Maps: OS Sheets Landranger 166; Pathfinder 1139.

A mainly woodland walk including a very attractive stretch of the Grand Union Canal.

Start At: 066982, the Clarendon Arms Inn, Chandlers Cross.

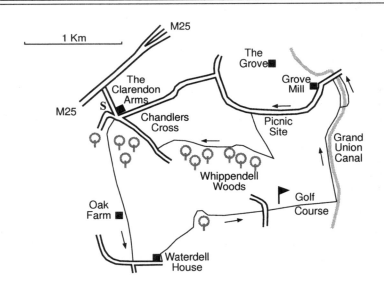

If you use the inn car park, please ask the landlord's permission beforehand. With your back to the inn's entrance, turn left along the main village road, soon turning right through a kissing gate. The narrow path beyond leads into Harrocks Wood: follow the prominent path through the wood, ignoring all turnings. Leave the wood along a narrow path between fields, passing Oak Farm on the right. Now ignore a path to the left, continuing ahead to a road (Little Green Lane, which seems to flood in all weathers). Turn left, passing Waterdell House and then immediately turning left along a signed path. After the Coachman's Cottage, continue along the path, going through a gate and turning right along the field edge. Follow the path around the field, to turn the corner of the Waterdell Spring woodland. Cross two stiles, continuing with a wire fence on your right. At the wood's corner, ignore a stile on the right and bear left across a field. Cross a stile, go through a small wood, then through a gap. Turn right, remaining in the field, and walk along the woodland edge. In the corner, go over a stile and cross the centre of the field beyond to reach a gate. Cross a lane and follow the path opposite uphill. At the top, cross West Herts Golf Course, going over a crossing track to reach another section of the course. Go downhill to reach the **Grand Union Canal**. Now ignore a path to the left and, just before the bridge, turn left by the lock to go along the towpath.

Follow the towpath for about a mile, passing two locks and crossing a footbridge on to the opposite bank. Go under a road bridge (No. 165) and turn right up steps to reach a road. Turn right, over a bridge, following the road for $^1/_2$ mile. Go over the River Gade and pass Grove Mill (now residential apartments) on the right. Continue uphill, with Grove Park on the right, and the substantial **The Grove** beyond. Near the top, by the blue width restriction sign turn left into a picnic site car park. At the far side, take the wide path by the metal gates, following it through **Whippendell Woods**, ignoring all turnings. On reaching a junction of paths in a clearing by some picnic tables, turn sharp right, downhill, passing a 'No Horses' sign. Go over a crossing track, maintaining direction, and then bearing right at a significant fork, leaving the original path to go uphill along a grassy track. Follow the track, ignoring all turnings, to reach a fork. Bear right, remaining in the trees and going slightly uphill to reach a lane (Rousebarn Lane). Turn right to return to Chandlers Cross.

POINTS OF INTEREST:

Grand Union Canal – The canal goes through Cassiobury Park owned, at the turn of the century when the canal was built, by the Earl of Essex. In 1800 the Earl demanded the building of the famous ornamental bridge just to the north of Grove Mill before he would allow the canal to run through his estate.

The Grove – This is a fine red-brick Georgian Mansion with an unfortunate corrugated iron roof. It once contained many art treasures and valuable paintings by such artists as Romney, Van Dyck, Gainsborough and Hogarth, but is now a training and management centre.

Whippendell Woods – The woods extend to over 200 acres. The mixed woodland, (oak, larch, beech, Scots pine and silver birch) is criss-crossed by footpaths. There are bluebells in Spring, a wide variety of Summer flowers and fungi in the Autumn. Nature Trails and Orienteering Maps are available from Watford Town Hall.

REFRESHMENTS:

The Clarendon Arms, Chandlers Cross.

Walk 77   **SARRATT** $5\frac{1}{2}$m ($8\frac{1}{2}$km)

Maps: OS Sheets Landranger 166; Pathfinder 1139 and 1119.

A rural walk, despite the closeness of the M25.

Start At: 043995, the Boot Inn, on the Green, Sarratt.

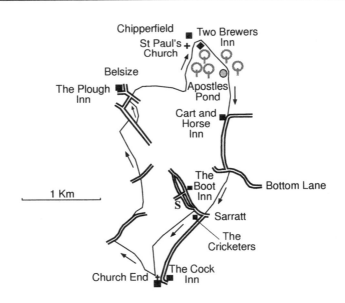

Facing the Boot Inn, turn right, after passing the Village Post Office, turn right down a path (Church End). Go through a parking area and cross a series of stiles along the left edges of fields, then enter a wood to reach a crossing track. Turn left through a kissing gate and follow the left edge, maintaining direction at the corner of a copse to head for the **Holy Cross Church**. The **Cock Inn** is on the left. Bear right in front of the church, keeping a holly hedge on your left. Cross a stile by a gate and ignore a path on the left, continuing along a wide track. Go through a gap and bear left to cross a stile in the hedge. Follow the left edge to cross a stile on to a lane. Turn right, uphill, and, after passing a farm drive on the right, turn left on to Dawes Common. Keep right at a fork, then bear right at the next fork to reach a crossing path. Turn left. At a path junction, turn left again, through a gate, and follow the left edge of a plantation.

Cross a stile and bear right to cross a stile in a hedge. Cross a lane and a stile, bearing right across the next field. Go over a pair of stiles in the corner, and bear right over a stile. Follow a wire fence on the left, cross a stile in the corner and turn right up a lane to reach a road. Turn right and, after 150 yards, turn left, immediately taking the left fork along path 21. Go over a crossing path and leave the wood over a stile. Bear right to a stile in a hedge. Turn right to a crossroads (the Plough Inn is to the left) and take the concrete track to the left of the telephone box. Where the concrete ends, bear right at the fork and follow a path for $^1/_2$ mile (Penman's Green). Go through a gate and, after 130 yards, turn left along a wood edge. Cross a stile on to Chipperfield Common. Cross a track and continue past a 'No Horse Riding' sign. Follow this path, ignoring all turnings, to reach a cricket pitch. Cross to the War Memorial and turn right through a parking area. Now bear right along a wide path, following it to **Twelve Apostles Pond**. Keep left of the pond and cross a stile by a gate. Follow a path through a kissing gate and continue along a lane, passing the Cart and Horse Inn. At the road, turn right towards Commonwood. After 500 yards, by Tudor House, fork left to reach Bottom Lane. Almost immediately go right over a stile signed for Sarratt Green. At the top of a climb go over a stile and follow a fenced path into a small housing estate. At the main road, turn right, passing the Cricketers Inn to reach the start.

POINTS OF INTEREST:

Holy Cross Church – This small, 12th-century church is built in the shape of a cross. The tower was rebuilt in the 15th century using Roman bricks. It is the only church in Hertfordshire to have a saddleback roof. It was restored in 1865 by Sir George Scott. **The Cock Inn** – In the 17th century, the inn was a mortuary for plague victims who, it is believed, were buried in the surrounding fields. The Inn is said to have an especially wide door so that the coffins could be stored inside. **Twelve Apostles Pond** – Originally a fish pond – a valuable source of food for the local Dominican friars before the Dissolution of the Monasteries – it was later called the Twelve Apostles, as it was surrounded by twelve lime trees planted in 1714. These trees have recently been felled, twelve new trees being planted to take their place. Close to the pond are a number of chestnut trees, the oldest perhaps 750 years old.

REFRESHMENTS:
The Boot Inn, Sarratt.
The Cricketers Inn, Sarratt.
The Plough Inn, Belsize.
The Two Brewers Inn, Chipperfield Common.
The Cart and Horse Inn, Commonwood.

Maps: OS Sheets Landranger 175; Explorer 3.

A walk through the Hambleden Valley visiting Luxters Brewery and Vineyard.

Start: At 785866, the public car park by the Stag and Huntsman Inn.

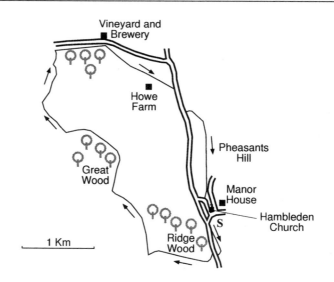

Turn left out of the car park, passing **Hambleden Church**. Cross the bridge and take the footpath on the left. Cross a stile on to a track and turn right to reach a road. Turn right along the road, then, beyond the last house, turn left up a track. At the top of the incline, ignore the path to the right, continuing ahead with views, to the left, of the Hambleden Valley and the River Thames.

At a crossing path, maintain direction, on a higher level, going downhill to reach a farm track. Continue ahead along the private road to reach a crossing path by a cattle trough, following the waymarker arrow. Go past a tumbledown, tin-roofed building on the right and bear right uphill to enter Great Wood. Do not be surprised to see deer or foxes on this stretch of the walk. At a crossing path, bear left, uphill, and, on reaching the path top, bear right for a further uphill stretch, follow a bridleway along a sunken path. If it is wet there is an alternative path on top of the bank. On emerging from the wood, continue ahead, following a path with a fence on the left. Continue uphill to reaching a crossing path. Be careful here: in the summer this path gets very overgrown and is difficult to spot. Cross the stile to the right and head for the gap in the fence, passing through a line of trees. Follow the field's left edge, then bear right to cross a stile, with a white marker post, into a wood. Follow the well-defined path to reach a road. Turn right: after passing an S-bend **Luxters Vineyard and Brewery** can be seen ahead.

Take the footpath in the left-hand corner of the brewery car park, going into a new plantation. As you leave the plantation the view into the Hambleden Valley is truly magnificent. Follow the path downhill, cross a stile and bear right to cross a stile in a hedge. Go down steps and head for a gate in the far corner of the field. Turn right along a road and then left down the lane with a post box on the corner. Cross a bridge and then go over a stile on the right. Now head for a stile in the hedge, cross it and turn right, soon continuing with a hedge on your left. Go through two gates, cross a road, and maintain direction along a path between houses. Go through a kissing gate into a field and walk with a hedge and gardens on your left. Cross a stile, go through a small stand of trees and several kissing gates, heading for Hambleden Church to reach a lane. Turn left and go through the churchyard. Now turn left along a road, passing the Stag and Huntsman Inn to return to the starting car park.

POINTS OF INTEREST:

Hambleden Church – The church, dedicated to St Mary, was begun in the 11th century. The east aisle was added in the 13th century, and the west tower in the 18th. The church was restored during in Victorian times. Interesting features include a Norman font, a wooden altar made from a bedhead said to have been used by Cardinal Wolsey, and a memorial to Sir Cope Doyley, his wife and ten children. In the graveyard WH Smith, the founder of the newsagent and stationery chain, is buried.

The Manor House – The House was once the home of the Earl of Cardigan, famous as the leader of the 'Charge of the Light Brigade' in the Crimean War. Now it is the home of Viscount Hambleden of the WH Smith family.

Old Luxters – The home of the Chiltern Valley Vineyard, Winery, Brewery and Gallery is open daily 10am – 6pm, but closes earlier in winter.

REFRESHMENTS:
The Stag and Huntsman Inn, Hambleden.

Maps: OS Sheets Landranger 165; Explorer 2.
A hilly walk to the summit of Lodge Hill.
Start: At 777021, between the church and the Lions Inn, Bledlow.

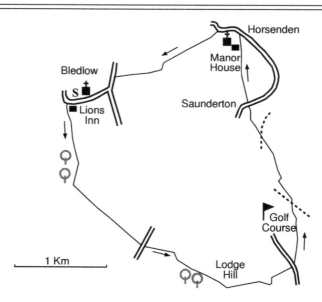

Bear left along the slip road towards the Lions Inn, passing the inn and turning sharp left along a wide track marked Swans Way. Ignore a turning to the right, continuing ahead, uphill, for about 1,000 yards to reach a Ridgeway National Trail marker post. Turn left and, after 30 yards, go through a kissing gate on the right, following the Ridgeway Trail. Bear left in this large undulating field, following the line of the fence on the left. Ignore a stile on the left, continuing ahead to go through a kissing gate in the field corner. Turn right, ignoring a stile on the right, and continuing with a hedge on your right. Go through a kissing gate, cross Wigan's Lane, and through the gate opposite. Cut across the corner of the field beyond, go through a gate and maintain direction across the next field. Go over a crossing track and, at the next gate, turn right. After 70 yards, follow a path into trees, starting the climb to the summit of Lodge Hill. Follow the clearly marked Ridgeway across the hill, descending through a series of gates. The going here can be slippery when wet. Nearing the bottom, in a field corner, ignore the path ahead, bearing left and keeping a hedge on your right. Turn right with the hedge line to reach a road.

Cross the road and follow the Ridgeway down a farm track. Keep right of an isolated house, cross the centre of a field and go through a kissing gate. Now follow a fenced path with a golf course on either side. Go through a kissing gate and cross a railway, with care. Go through a small plantation and another gate, here leaving the Ridgeway, turning left and keeping the railway fence on your left. Bear slightly away from the fence, along the line of a bank, cross a stile and continue along a tarmac drive, keeping the Old Rectory on your right. Cross a road and go through a gap in a hedge. Follow the left edge of the field beyond, and, in the corner, go through a white gate and recross the railway. Follow the left edge of the next field, heading for the houses in Saunderton. Cross a road and go up the drive of Brook Cottage, soon following a narrow, fenced path to go through a kissing gate. The path beyond follows the line of a stream on the left: cross a stile and go through a gate to reach a stile on to a road by the drive to Horsenden House. Turn left, crossing a bridge and passing the church on the left. At the T-junction, cross the stile by a gate and continue along the left edge of a field. Cross a stile and a stream, and continue ahead along a raised path. Cross a track and continue with a hedge on your right. Go through a gap in the corner and turn left along a bridle way. After 50 yards, turn right over a stile and follow the left field edge to cross a stile into a yard. Go along a tarmac drive, passing Plum Tree Cottage to reach a road. Turn left and, after 150 yards, turn right along Church End, passing a gate for **Lyde Garden** and **Holy Trinity Church** on the way back to the start.

POINTS OF INTEREST:

Lyde Garden – This water garden has been cleverly designed with raised walkways over pools of clear water surrounded by almost tropical vegetation. The gardens, which are open to the public, were a gift to the village by the Carrington family who own the Manor House opposite the entrance. The manner in which the water seems to gush from under the church, led to a local rhyme attributed to Mother Shipton – 'They that live and do abide, Shall see the church fall in the Lyde'.

Holy Trinity Church – The church dates back to Norman times, making something of a mockery of the local rhyme. Inside there are early examples of wall paintings and glass, and an 18th-century altar.

REFRESHMENTS:
The Lions Inn, Bledlow.

Walk 80 **HILL END AND THE GRAND UNION** 6m (9km)
Maps: OS Sheets Landranger 176; Pathfinder 1139.
A pleasant walk in the Colne Valley.
Start: At 043929, Springwell Lock car park.

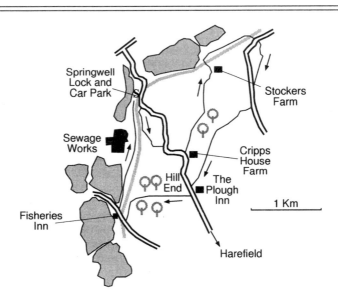

To reach Springwell Lane, turn off A412 Denham to Rickmansworth road. From the
car park, cross the canal bridge and turn right, going uphill around a sweeping left-
hand bend. Just before reaching a drive, turn right along a path between wire fences.
Cross a stile on to a wide drive and turn left along a track, keeping the barns on your
right. After a pair of barns on the left, ignore a stile ahead and bear left, uphill. Near
the top, bear left, passing between Springwell Farm and some open barns, to reach a
lane. Turn right, and ignore a path on the right to continue uphill. Now, by Cripps
Farm Bungalow, turn left over a stile and follow a grass track between hedges to
reach a gate. Go through, bear right and, soon, skirt around the left edge of Cooks
Wood. At the corner of the wood, follow the fence line to a stile. Cross and follow the
left field edge to a stile in the corner. Cross and bear left along a track towards **Stockers
Farm**. At the wooden gate, turn right over a stile, then cross two more stiles to reach

a farm track. Turn left through a parking area then right to cross the canal bridge. Turn right along the towpath by Stockers Lock.

Follow the towpath for about $^3/_4$ mile, passing the Aquadrome on your left. At the next bridge (No. 174), climb to the road and cross the canal. At the junction, turn left and, after 100 yards, take a signed path on the right. Go through a barrier, up some steps and turn right. Now bear right along Sherfield Avenue. After 150 yards, turn left along a path between houses. Cross a stile and turn right along a track. Go through the corner of the wood, keeping right at a fork. Follow the path along the edge of the wood, with a new golf course on your left. At the end of the golf course, cross a stile and go though a small wood. Continue downhill to cross a stile on to a road. Turn left, but soon turn right along a path by the entrance to Fieldways Farm. Ignore a path on the left, continuing along the track towards the farm. Leave the track at the farm entrance, going ahead along the right edge of a field. Cross a stile and the centre of the field beyond. Go over a footbridge, cross a stile and follow the right edge of the next field. Cross two stiles and pass well to the left of White Heath Farm. Go over a stile and through a cul-de-sac to reach a lane. Turn left, passing the Plough Inn, in Hill End village, and, after 60 yards, turn right along a path between fences. Follow the path through Park Wood, leaving past a barrier and continuing along a tarmac track to reach a lane. Turn left, passing the old **Coppermill** on the right, to reach a road. Turn right, negotiating the bend with care, and cross the canal bridge by the Fisheries Inn. Turn right along the **Grand Union Canal** towpath (between the River Colne and the canal) for a pleasant walk of about a mile to return to Springwell Lock.

POINTS OF INTEREST:

Stockers Farm— This fine, 16th-century farm was used for the filming of the television series *Black Beauty*.

Coppermill – The mill, built in 1803, has been used for milling corn, paper and copper. Sheet copper was produced here for the bottoms of Royal Naval ships and also for the dome of St Paul's Cathedral.

Grand Union Canal – The canal was completed in 1803 and originally named the Grand Junction. Some mileage plaques still bear the initials GJC Co. The building of the canal was a major feat of craft and hard work. All the digging was carried out by pick and shovel, the many tons of rock and earth being moved by horse and cart.

REFRESHMENTS:

The Fisheries Inn, Coppermill Lock.
The Plough, Hill End.

Walk 81 **WALKERN** 6m (9km)

Maps: OS Sheets Landranger 166; Pathfinder 1073.

Easy walk with views of the Beane Valley.

Start: At 289263, Main Street, Walkern, opposite the Robin Hood or Yew Tree Inns.

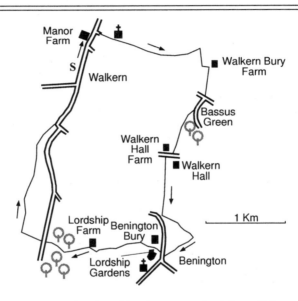

Facing the inns turn left, passing the White Lion Inn, on the right, and Manor Farm on the left. Go past the United Reform Church and turn right down Church End. Keep to the raised path to cross a ford and pass **St Mary the Virgin Church** on the left. Where the road bends right, continue ahead, ignoring all turnings. Bear left at a pair of cottages, then bear right at the next fork. Follow the track through open fields to reach a T-junction. Turn right, with Walkern Bury Farm on the left. At the next T-junction, take the second on the left, to bear right in front of a brick barn, beside a storage barn (the ancient Ring and Bailey is on the left here). Continue down the rough track, following it through the small hamlet of Bassus Green. At the crossroads, continue ahead along a road signed for Clay End. Ignore a path on the right and continue to the edge of a wood. Turn right along a bridleway following the woodland edge. Cross a stream and go uphill towards Walkern Hall Farm to reach a lane. Turn right and, after 50 yards, turn left along a bridleway. Walkern Hall can be seen to the left. Go through a metal gate and along a concrete drive. Before the last cottage, turn left, keeping to the right edge of a field. Go through a gap in the hedge on the right, and turn right down a track. Ignore a bridleway on the left, but turn left at a lane. Immediately turn right through a kissing gate, cross the centre of the paddock and two stiles to reach Duck Lane. Turn right into Benington. At the crossroads, the Bell Inn is to the left, the church is ahead, while to the right are the **Lordship Gardens** and castle remains. Turn right up Walkern Road and, soon, left through a kissing gate. Cross a stile and the centre of a field. Go over a ladder stile and a footbridge and stile, continuing along the right edge of a field. Go past a pond to reach a stile in the field corner, keeping left of Lordship Farm. Go through a metal gate and continue ahead, passing between barns. Follow a path to the left, cross a stile and go along the edge of Hally Park Wood. Go through a gap and cross a stile on to a road. Take the path opposite, crossing the field centre. Cross a footbridge, turn left, and immediately right along the left edge of a field. Bear slightly right to cross a stile 30 yards from the field corner. Follow the line of the winding stream, crossing five stiles. Now cross a stile to the left of a marker post, going along the right edge of the next field. Cross a stile into a paddock, with an old flour mill (1881) on the right. At a road, turn left and, at the crossroads go ahead into **Walkern**.

POINTS OF INTEREST:
St Mary the Virgin Church – This was originally a wooden Anglo-Saxon church and is the oldest in Hertfordshire. It was built of flint in the 11th century and incorporates features from every century since then. A Saxon Rood Cross, one of only three surviving in England, can be seen inside.
Lordship Gardens, Benington – Open Wednesday and Sunday during the summer.
Walkern – The village is mentioned in the Domesday Book as Walcha. According to legend the first site chosen for a church was at Box near Stevenage. When the foundation stones were laid, they were moved through the air each night by the devil shouting 'Walk on ! Walk on !'. Hence the current village name of Walkern. The village was the home of Jane Wenham, the last woman to be convicted of witchcraft by a jury, in 1712. She was granted a pardon by the Queen and, too frightened to live in the village, spent her last days peacefully in Hertingfordbury.

REFRESHMENTS:
There are inns in Walkern and Benington, as mentioned in the text.

Maps: OS Sheets Landranger 166; Pathfinder 1119.
Field paths out, with a return along the Grand Union towpath.
Start: At 016035, the Bull Inn, Bovingdon.

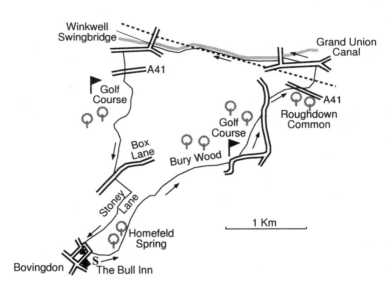

Take the road to the side of the Bull Inn, heading towards **St Lawrence's Church**. Turn left along a path through the churchyard and, on leaving, turn right, following the road to the right. At the right-hand bend, go ahead, over a stile and follow a path signed for Bury Wood. Cross two stiles and bear left to a stile in the top left corner. Now ignore a path to the right, continuing ahead, with a hedge on your left. Go past a small copse, Homefield Spring, on the left and, after passing the rear gardens of houses, cross a stile on the wood edge and turn left along a path beside the wood. Ignore a path into the wood, maintaining direction to pass a clump of trees in the field. Now bear right across the field corner, go through a gap in the hedge and continue to cross a stile on to a lane. Walk ahead, following the lane past Felden Barns and a private road, on the left, then go through a kissing gate, also on the left, and follow the left edge of the field beyond. Cross a stile in the corner and go through two kissing gates.

Go over a crossing track and through a kissing gate. On reaching a tarmac track, turn right, taking care as you cross the golf course, to reach a road. Turn left, taking extra care as this short stretch of road is without a footpath. Before the left bend, turn right along a bridle way. Ignore a path on the left and, at the next fork, bear left, downhill. Go over a crossing path and bear right as you leave Roughdown Common to cross the footbridge over the A41. Ignore a path to the right, continuing downhill. Bear left at a T-junction, crossing the railway to reach the main road. Turn left and cross the road, with care, at a garage. Go through a swing gate, bearing left to reach a canal bridge by the Fishery Inn. Turn left along the towpath, following it to reach the Winkwell swing bridge by the Three Horseshoes Inn. With the swing bridge on your right, turn left over a brick bridge and follow a narrow lane to the main road. Turn right and, after 500 yards, cross, with care, and turn left, opposite Bourne End Hall, along an uphill path. Go through a swing gate and cross a footbridge over the A41 to reach a golf course. Go ahead, towards a small wood, following its edge to reach Westbrook Hay. Bear right to follow the fence (with it on your left), then go along a rough track. Before the driving range, ignore a path to the right, following the road past the clubhouse. After 200 yards, at a path marker, turn left into a wood. At the road (the B4505), turn right, and, almost immediately, left down Bushfield Road. At the T-junction with Stoney Lane, turn right and follow the lane to the church in **Bovingdon**, reversing the outward route back to the start.

POINTS OF INTEREST:

St Lawrence's Church – The first church in Bovingdon was built on this site in 1235. The present church was completely rebuilt in 1841-46, though part of the tower survives from an earlier building. The churchyard is one of the largest in Hertfordshire. The avenue of yew trees (a very poisonous tree) are said to have been planted to prevent the vicar from grazing his animals in the churchyard.

Bovingdon – Once only a small village with a population of 500, Bovingdon has grown substantially, increasing tenfold over the last fifty years. In earlier times there was a thriving cottage industry of straw plaiting for the local hat industry at Luton. During the 1939-45 War the local airfield was used by both the RAF and the American Airforce, bombers leaving the airfield for Germany at a rate of one every two minutes.

REFRESHMENTS:

The Fishery Inn, Felden.
The Three Horseshoes Inn, Winkwell.
The Bull, Bovingdon.
The Wheatsheaf, Bovingdon.

Walk 83 **TINGEWICK** 6m (9km)

Maps: OS Sheets Landranger 165 and 152; Pathfinder 1046.

A walk for the more adventurous, along seldom walked field paths and at the time of writing often overgrown and unmarked. The Pathfinder Map is almost a must.

Start: At 655328, the car park at the Village Hall, Tingewick.

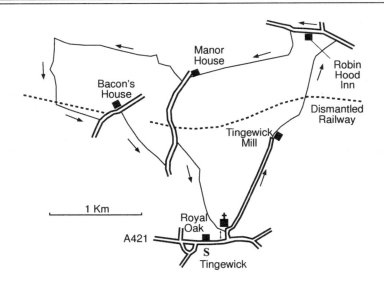

Facing the Royal Oak Inn, turn right and, soon, left, up Church Lane. Turn right in front of the church and keep to the right of St Mary's Court. Now ignore a path to the right, continuing ahead along a straight, narrow lane for a mile to reach **Tingewick Mill**. Go through the mill gates, and between buildings to reach a gate. Go through and cross a footbridge. Cross another footbridge and bear left to a hedge corner. Bear right and walk with a hedge on your left, then 100 yards before the field corner, go left through a gap and bear left to the stile opposite. Climb steps and cross a dismantled railway. Cross a stile and bear right, with a hedge and stream on your right. Go through a gap and turn right to a stile in front of a footbridge. (Do not cross the stile on the right.) Cross the bridge and turn left, soon leaving the fence to bear right to a ladder stile. Cross and bear right, heading for the second telegraph pole from the left. Bear left and go through a gate to reach a lane. Turn left, passing the Robin Hood Inn and, after 150 yards (beyond a gravel track), turn left along a field edge, with a hedge on your left. At present there is an absence of stiles and footpath signs here. In the corner, turn right along the field edge, soon going over the fence and following the hedge on the right. Cross a metal fence and continue along the right edge to a gate. Cross the footbridge beyond, turn left and, in the corner, turn right, uphill, and go over a stile. In the left corner of the next (divided) field, go over a footbridge, cross two stiles and go through a swing gate. Cross a stile in the corner and turn left along a road by Manor Farm. After 40 yards, turn right down a lane and, at the left bend, turn right through a kissing gate. Cross the field centre to a fork by a stand of trees. Bear left and, at a crossing track, turn right. After 100 yards, turn left along a bridleway. Go through a gap in a hedge, ignore a track on the right and cross a stream, continuing with a hedge on the right. When the hedge ends, turn left, cross the field and go through a gate in the corner. Go into a small group of trees and turn left over a footbridge. Follow a path to cross the **dismantled railway** and, at the three-way fork, turn sharp left along a hedge. Soon leave the hedge, bear right to a gate on to a lane. Turn left, then right opposite **Bacon's House**. Go through a gate and into a small wood. Leave through a gap and cross a field. Go through two gates and turn left along a road. At the drive to Rectory Farm, turn right over a stile and bear right, heading just left of the top right corner. Cross two stiles, follow the hedge on the right, and cross a stile to the right of a storage barn. Go over a track, cross three stiles and bear left across a field. Go through a kissing gate and along a path to reach Church Lane. Turn right to the start.

POINTS OF INTEREST:
Tingewick Mill – First recorded in the Domesday Book as being worth four shillings. The mill ceased working in 1966, though some of the machinery is still in place. Until the 1930s eel traps were common here, the eels being sent to Billingsgate Market.
The Buckingham and Brackley Junction Railway – The railway was completed in 1850. As late as 1956 a halt was built at Water Stratford, with the railway being selected for a 'railcar' experiment. The olive green cars operated between Buckingham and Banbury. The line was closed in the early 1960s.
Bacon's House – Reputedly the house – part of the buildings of Home Farm – was owned by Sir Francis Bacon, the English statesman and philosopher.

REFRESHMENTS:
The Royal Oak, Tingewick.

Maps: OS Sheets Landranger 165; Explorer 2.
Walking among the rich farm land north of Aylesbury.
Start: At 806191, in the village of Hardwick.

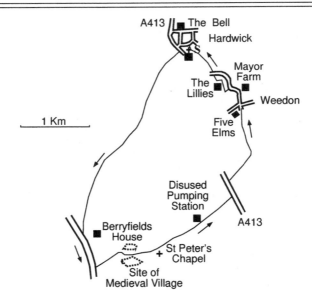

Return to the main road (the A413) with **St Mary's Church** on your left. Turn left and, after a few yards, cross, with care, to turn right over a stile. Cross the centre of the field beyond and, on reaching a fork, bear left and go over a crossing path. Continue ahead at the field boundary, keeping a hedge on your right. Go over a stile and continue along the hedge on the right. Cross a footbridge and go through a gate in the corner. Now leave the line of the brook, to go uphill along a well-defined cattle track. Cross the stile to the left of the most prominent electricity post and bear right across the field beyond. In the corner, cross a stile and turn left along a road. Go past Berryfields House, on the left, and after about 600 yards, cross a stile on the left. Cross the centre of a field, bearing right in the top corner to cross a stile by a pair of metal gates. Go along a gravel track. (There is an application pending for the diversion of some footpaths in this area – in fact some new stiles and footbridges have been erected. The new paths will be clearly signed when approved.) You are now crossing the site of a medieval village, with still clearly visible earthworks. Cross a concrete footbridge, staying on the track. Go past more earthworks, on the right, and the remains of St Peter's Chapel, continuing into the field corner. Cross a stile and follow the track past a disused pumping station on the left to reach the A413. Cross, with care, and turn left. After 300 yards, turn right through a gap and follow the left field edge. Ignore a stile on the left, bearing left at the hedge corner to go through a gate, now heading for the village of **Weedon**. Cross two stiles on to a tarmac track and go past two pretty thatched cottages and the Five Elms Inn to reach a crossroads.

Go ahead, up High Street, bearing left along the road in front of Manor Farm House (dated 1649). At the right-hand bend, turn left along a path. Go through a wooden gate and then turn right in front of a metal gate. Cross a stile and go through a short avenue of chestnut trees, passing **The Lillies** on the left. Cross a stile and bear right, continuing with the red-brick wall on your right. Bear right to go down steps and turn left by Lillies Farm (dated 1870, and with very ornate plasterwork to the front and side). Now, just before the drive to The Lillies (there is a statue on the left), turn right through a kissing gate. Go through a gate and cross a road to a stile. Go through an area of scrub and cross a footbridge. Bear left towards the church, crossing a stile in the corner. Turn right in the churchyard, leaving by an alley on the right to return to the village centre.

POINTS OF INTEREST:

St Mary's Church, Hardwick – The church is of Saxon origin, the north wall of the nave being pre-Norman. In the churchyard is a monument erected by Lord Nugent in 1818, beneath which are the re-interred remains of 247 bodies, victims of the Civil War battle of Aylesbury, fought at Holman's Bridge in 1642.

Weedon – The village has the distinction of having been the first place in Buckinghamshire licensed for Methodist services. John Wesley himself is said to have preached from a mound near the crossroads.

The Lillies – Re-built in the mid-19th century for Lord Nugent, MP for Aylesbury, the younger brother of the Duke of Buckingham. The Fleur-de-Lys symbol of the French royal family was retained in the porch as a reminder that Louis Philippe at one time considered spending his time in exile at the house. Baron Rothschild stayed at The Lillies in 1874 awaiting completion of Waddesdon Manor.

REFRESHMENTS:
The Bell Inn, Hardwick.
The Five Elms Inn, Weedon.

Maps: OS Sheets Landranger 165; Explorer 2.
Northchurch Common and the Grand Union Canal towpath.
Start: At 993082, Berkhamsted Station.

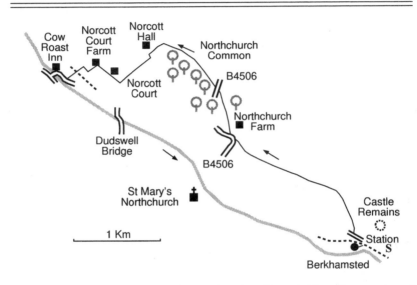

Facing the station, turn right and go under the railway bridge. The remains of
Berkhamsted Castle are on the right. Turn left down Bridgewater Road and then
first right along Castle Hill Avenue. Just before the road bends left, bear right, uphill,
along a well-defined path. At a road, bear left. Ignore Murray Road and Castle Gateway
and continue along a rough track, passing Castle Hill Farm. Ignore a path on the right,
then bear right after a storage barn and cross a stile. Keep to the left field edge, ignoring
a stile on the left, to cross a stile. Maintain direction along a fenced path beside the
playing fields, go over a crossing path and through the metal barrier, continuing along
a gravel track. At the crossroads continue ahead, downhill, to reach a road (the B4506).
Turn right, ignore the bridle way on the right, and go past Northchurch House on the
left. After 100 yards, opposite the Coach House, turn right along a track to Northchurch
Farm. After 200 yards, at a footpath marker post, turn left, leaving the track to head
into the centre of Northchurch Common. Go ahead at the bridleway marker post, with

good views to the left across the National Trust owned Common towards Wigginton. Bear left at a fork, cross the B4056, with care, and continue ahead, initially going downhill. Go over two crossing paths and, on reaching open fields, turn left. Ignore all paths to the left to go through a gap in the bushes, continuing with a wooded section of the Common on your left. At the wood corner, ignore the path marked' No Horses' and take the next left (a bridleway). On reaching a tarmac road, with Norcott Hall on the right, go ahead, downhill along the tarmac lane. Near the foot of the hill, turn right along a lane, passing the gates to Norcott Court on the right. Ignore a turning to the left (signed 'Main Road') continuing along the gravel track. Before the gates to Norcott Court Farm, bear left. Cross a stile by a metal gate and bear right to follow a track. After 100 yards, turn left through a hedge gap and cross the railway footbridge. Cross a stile and turn right along a lane to reach the canal, with the **Cow Roast Inn** ahead. Turn right before crossing the canal bridge and go back under the bridge to take the left-hand towpath. Follow the towpath to Dudswell Lock (No. 48). There, cross the bridge over the canal and turn left along the right-hand towpath, so maintaining direction. As you go under Northchurch bridge there are good views of **St Mary's Church** on the right. On reaching Berkhamsted, go under a wooden footbridge and past the tennis courts on the left. After the next lock (Station 53) go up the steps before the bridge and cross the bridge, continuing ahead to reach the station.

POINTS OF INTEREST:

Berkhamsted Castle – Berkhamsted was a prosperous wool town in the Middle Ages, having been originally important because of its Norman castle and its links with William the Conqueror. The castle had many owners until 1495, when it was abandoned and fell into ruin, some of the stones being used for other buildings in the town.

Cow Roast Inn – Once known as the Cow Rest, the inn had large pens for the cattle to rest when drovers from the Midlands were on their way to the London markets.

St Mary's Church, Northchurch – The church, dating back to Saxon times, is the oldest in the area and has several attractive features. The churchyard contains the grave of Peter the Wild Boy, who died in 1785. He was brought to England by Queen Caroline in 1725 after he had been found wandering wild in a forest in Germany. He was entrusted to a Northchurch farmer and in view of his wandering habits a collar was placed around his neck detailing his address. The collar is now in Berkhamsted school.

REFRESHMENTS:
The Cow Roast Inn, on the Grand Union Canal.
There is a wide variety of possibilities in Berkhamsted.

Walk 86   **GREAT HAMPDEN**   6m (9¹/₂km)

Maps: OS Sheets Landranger 165; Explorer 2.

A superb half-day's walk with a wide variety of scenery.

Start: At 846015, Hampden Common, on the road opposite the cricket pitch.

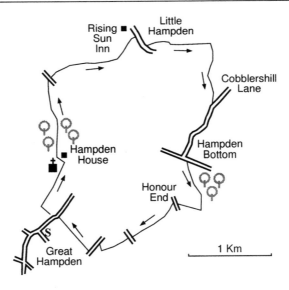

Return to the main road and turn right, passing the Hampden Arms Inn. After the last cottage on the right, cross the road and cross a stile on to a footpath. Follow the field's left edge and bear left through a clump of trees. Turn right along a crossing path, cross a track and go through a kissing gate, then take a left fork and continue through several kissing gates to reach the church yard of **Great Hampden Church**. Opposite **Hampden House**, turn left through a gate and immediately go right over a stile. Bear left, passing the front elevation of Hampden House, then cross a stile into woodland, following the fenced path. Leave the wood over a stile and continue along the valley bottom. Cross a stile, a minor road and another stile on to a footpath, following it through a small wood, soon going uphill. Ignore a crossing path and continue uphill to another crossing path. Turn right into a field, heading for a gap in the trees. Beyond the trees, cross the centre of the next field, go over a crossing track and continue ahead, down a gravel track, to reach a road. The Rising Sun Inn is to the left here.

Turn right, then left on to a footpath marked for the South Bucks Way. Cross a parking area and go over a stile. Follow the track, beyond downhill through woodland and, after 90 yards, bear right along the South Bucks Way. Leave the wood and follow a field edge, then go uphill with the hedge on your left. Cross a stile, going steeply uphill and bearing right through scrub. Nearing the top, at a crossing path, turn right. Cross two stiles, following the waymarked path into woodland. Now bear right, downhill to reach a lane (Cobblers Hill Lane). Turn right, downhill, to reach the road at Hampden Bottom. Turn left, then cross the road to reach a footpath opposite Lower Honour End. Cross a stile and 'The Glade', keeping a wire fence on your right. Go over a stile and follow the edge of wood. At a crossing path, continue ahead, then ignore a turn to the left, but bear right at the next fork. At the next waymarked crossing, turn right to reach a five way crossing. Turn immediately right, crossing a stile and the centre of the field beyond. Cross a stile, a paddock and another stile on to a lane. Cross, go through a gate and up a short concrete path to another gate. Turn left across a field, heading for a metal gate. Go through and turn immediately right through another gate. (The waymarking of these paths is not very obvious). Cross a stile in the field corner and maintain direction, heading for a wood. Bear left into the wood and then walk down to a road. Cross and follow the path opposite uphill. Leave the wood to enter a field and continue to a crossing track just beyond a single oak tree. Turn right and go across a field to reach a lane. Turn left and, after 100 yards, take the footpath on the right. Follow this path all the way through to Great Hampden village, reaching a road. Turn left and, after passing the Hampden Arms, turn left to reach the start.

POINTS OF INTEREST:

Great Hampden Church – Dedicated to St Mary Magdalen, the church was built in the 13th century. It houses some early 16th-century benches with linenfold panelling. Of most interest are the Hampden family monuments and some very fine brasses.

Hampden House – Built on the hill overlooking the two Hampdens, this was once the home of John Hampden, a cousin of Oliver Cromwell. Best remembered for his stand against the imposition of the Ship Tax, Hampden was wounded in the Battle of Chalgrove Field and buried at Great Hampden.

REFRESHMENTS:

The Hampden Arms, Great Hampden.
The Rising Sun, Little Hampden Common.

Walk 87   **OLD AMERSHAM**   6m (9$^1/_2$km)

Maps: OS Sheets Landranger 165 and 175; Explorer 3.

An undulating walk below the historic town of Amersham.

Start: At 962973, the public car park off the A 355, by the Tesco
supermarket.

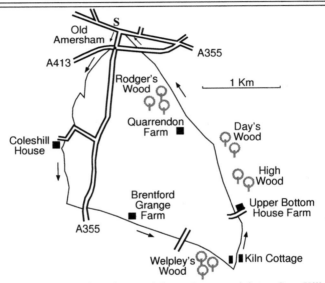

From the car park, turn left to the roundabout, then turn right up Gore Hill to reach
another roundabout. Turn right along a tarmac path and cross a footbridge. Now, on
reaching the rear gardens of some houses, turn right along a fenced path. Where the
gardens end, take the grass track along the valley for 600 yards, then go through a gap
in the hedge to reach a path with a hedge to its left. The path climbs past a white
cottage, then passes between hedges and trees to reach a road. Turn right and, at a
sharp right hand bend, cross the stile ahead, by a metal gate. **Coleshill House** is to the
right here. Cross a stile and continue along the left edge of a field. Cross a double stile
and walk downhill with a hedge on your left. Now, where the hedge bears left, continue
ahead along a grassy track. On reaching a gap in a hedge and a crossing path, turn left
towards the road to reach the corner of the field. Bear right to go through a gap, cross
a footbridge and go up steps to the road (the A355).

Cross the road, with care, to a stile. Cross and follow the path beyond uphill, walking with a hedge on your right. As the path levels out, you will see Brentford Grange Farm ahead. Just before the farm, go through a gap in the hedge and cross two stiles, ignoring a footbridge on the right. Continue ahead to reach a stile in the left field corner. Cross this, a driveway and another stile and follow the path beyond along the left edge of a field. Cross a stile in the corner and continue ahead over a series of stiles to reach a lane. Cross the lane and the stile opposite and, on reaching an unused stile on edge of the field beyond, bear right, following the direction of the waymarker arrow across the centre of the field, keeping Welpley's Wood on your right. Go through a gap in a hedge, cross a stile and turn left along a farm track, soon passing Kiln Cottage. Follow the track downhill to reach a road at Upper Bottom House Farm. Turn right at the farm and left at the end of the barns. Go up steps and cross a stile, then bear right to reach a line of trees and a wire fence. Turn right to cross a stile in the field corner, then bear left to cross another stile. Bear right to cross a stile in the field corner, keeping Day's Wood on your right. Cross a stile and immediately turn left to pass Quarrendon Farm, on the left. Where the hedge bears left towards the farm, bear right across the centre of the field and, at the hedge corner, bear right towards the wood. Cross a stile to cut across the wood corner, crossing another stile to leave the wood. Bear left to reach a gap in a hedge, go through and head for the stile in line with the bypass bridge. Cross the stile and turn left, soon joining a tarmac path and following it under the bypass. Bear left, keeping to the farm track and cross a cattle grid. Now turn right and cross a stile on to the main road, turning left to return to the start in **Amersham**.

POINTS OF INTEREST:

Amersham – Amersham High Street is one of the finest town streets in the Chilterns, lined either side with 17th- and 18th-century buildings. St Mary's Church dates back to the early 12th century, but was heavily restored in 1890. Inside the Drake Chapel there are many attractive brasses and monuments. William Drake gave the town the Market Hall, built in 1682, which protrudes into the High Street, and another William had the Almshouses built in 1657. Several fine coaching inns on either side of the town hall are still prospering today.

Coleshill House – This simply designed Georgian building was enlarged and remodelled in Italianate style in 1850. It has now been converted to upmarket flats.

REFRESHMENTS:

There are places to suit all tastes in Amersham.

Maps OS Sheets Landranger 166; Pathfinder 1120.

To the south of the surprisingly quiet village of Northaw. There is some road walking, but the views from Hemps Hill are excellent.

Start: At 278023, St Thomas of Canterbury Church, Northaw.

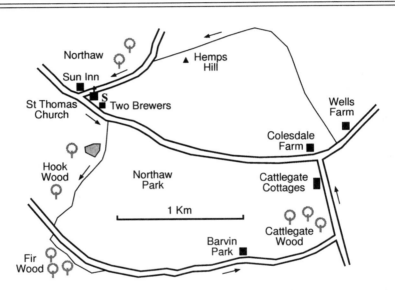

Return to the main road and turn left, passing the Post Office and the Two Brewers Inn. After 150 yards turn right down a tarmac track (Hook Lane). The track soon changes to loose gravel: continue to the bottom. Here the path narrows: continue ahead, going over a brick bridge and passing the Northaw Fishery Lake. Continue uphill, then bear right along a concrete track, with terraced cottages on the right, to reach a minor road at **Fir Wood**. Cross the road and the stile opposite, and turn left along a woodland path running parallel to the road. Pass a small pond and continue along the meandering path. The M25 motorway can be seen and heard on the right. Go over a stile to enter a more open wooded area, still with the minor road on the left. The path bears right to reach a stile: do not cross, bearing left to leave the wood and to rejoin the road. Turn right and follow the road, with care. There is a grass verge but it can be very overgrown. After $^3/_4$ mile you will pass St Raphael's Barvin Park which was once a hospital, but was recently sold, possibly for residential development. Now ignore a path on the right, continuing along the road, passing Cattlegate Wood, on the left, to reach a T-junction. Turn left and cross the road to the grass verge. This road should be walked with great care as it can be very busy. Re-cross the road to the pavement outside Cattlegate Cottages and continue to a T-junction.

Turn right and, at the bottom of the dip, cross a stile on the left, by a pair of metal gates. Go along the driveway to the Colesdale Farm shop, with the Northaw Book on your right. Go over four stiles in succession, maintaining direction, with Northaw Church on the skyline to the left. The area immediately on the left is part of the Northaw point to point racecourse where an annual meeting is held on Spring Bank Holiday Monday. Where the gravel track bends to the right, ignore a kissing gate on the right and immediately turn left, before the pair of metal gates, to go along a narrow path with a wire fence on the right. Go over a footbridge and a stile, and continue ahead going uphill to reach a stile. Cross, go through a hedge gap and cross another stile, continuing with a wire fence on your right. Go over two stiles and continue with the hedge line on the left, going downhill. Cross the stile to the left of a metal gate on to a road and turn left, passing some large, established houses and the primary school to return to **St Thomas of Canterbury Church**.

POINTS OF INTEREST:

Fir and Pond Woods – The woods are a Nature Reserve managed by the Herts and Middlesex Wildlife Trust. The woodland is a remnant section of the Enfield Chase, an ancient royal hunting forest which, at one time, covered almost 20,000 acres. Within the woods there is a variety of different habitats supporting an abundance of wildlife. The two adjoining woods survive from medieval times when the country was far more open than it is today, with areas of woodland intermixed with areas of grass and heath. During the 1650s many trees were felled to fuel the English Civil Wars, then, in 1777, Enfield Chase was divided up and sold into private ownership.

St Thomas of Canterbury, Northaw – The church was rebuilt in 1881, by C Kirk & Sons of Sleaford, after a fire destroyed the original building. All that remains of the previous church is a 15th-century octagonal font which can be seen in the churchyard near the south door of the nave.

REFRESHMENTS:
The Sun Inn, Northaw.
The Two Brewers, Northaw.

Walk 89   LACEY GREEN   6m (10km)

Maps: OS Sheets Landranger 165; Explorer 2.

A visit to the restored Lacey Green Windmill and peaceful Monkton Wood.

Start: At 828019, opposite the Pink and Lily Inn.

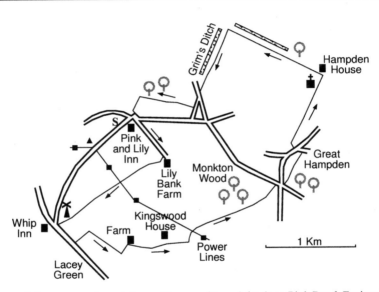

To reach the start, go through Lacey Green and turn right along Pink Road. Facing the **Pink and Lily Inn**, take the lane to the left – Lily Bottom Lane. After 600 yards, at the bottom, turn right along a bridleway. Near the top of the hill, turn right over a stile, (be careful not to miss this – it lies in a gap between the trees) and cross the field beyond, bearing left to reach a stile in the hedge. Cross and head for a gap between a pylon and **Lacey Green Windmill**. Maintain direction, crossing several stiles, to reach a road, passing the windmill on your right. Now, with the Whip Inn on your right, turn left towards Lacey Green village. After 400 yards, by the house 'Byways', turn left along a track. After the last house on the left, turn right into a field. In the corner, go through a gap on to a gravel track and, after 30 yards, turn left, downhill. At the gates to White House Farm, bear right, continuing along the track and ignoring paths on either side. Ignore another crossing path and continue along the valley bottom, passing Kingswood House. After a further 350 yards, turn left along an uphill path by the edge of a wood. Ignore a stile to the left, continuing uphill to emerge on to a narrow path. At a crossing path, continue ahead into Monkton Wood.

Go through a wooden gate, pass a tree with a five arrow waymarker and continue to a wooden gate where a footpath goes left and a bridleway goes right. Keep left along the footpath following it for $\frac{1}{2}$ mile to reach a road. Bear right, cross a junction and then go left over a stile. Walk uphill into Hampden Coppice, bearing left at a fork and going over a stile on to Hampden Common. Cross the Common's left side to reach a road. Turn left to reach a junction by the Hampden Arms Inn. Cross the road to the milepost and go ahead along a tarmac drive. Where the drive bears left, continue ahead, through a gate, and cross the field beyond. Cross a farm track and go through a gap to reach a kissing gate. Bear left and go through a series of kissing gates, heading for Great Hampden Church. Bear left in the churchyard, to join a road opposite Hampden House. Turn left, go through a wooden gate and continue ahead to go through another gate to reach the corner of a wood. Note the ancient earthworks, Grim's Ditch, on the right. At a crossing path turn left, still with Grim's Ditch on your right. The path is waymarked through the trees and along a field edge. Cross a stile on to a road and take the minor road opposite, signposted for Lacey Green. After the road bends left and right, turn right along a footpath into woodland. At a crossing path, bear slightly left along a wide track following the waymarkers. After passing a stile on the left, at the next crossing path, turn left, go through a small swing gate and turn left along a gravel track. Follow the track to a road and turn right to regain the start.

POINTS OF INTEREST:

Pink and Lily Inn – The name is derived from Mr. Pink and Miss Lily, domestic servants at Hampden House who married and set up house. It has a literary connection, as Rupert Brooke, the poet, often frequented the inn.

Lacey Green Windmill – The windmill stands back from the road at the highest point of the village. Built in 1650, it is believed to be the country's oldest surviving smock mill. It was originally located in Chesham, being moved in its present location in 1821. It operated until 1915, then fell into disrepair, but was restored in 1971 by the Chiltern Society. It is open on summer Sunday and Bank Holiday afternoons.

REFRESHMENTS:

Pink and Lily Inn, at the start.
The Whip Inn, Lacey Green.
The Hampden Arms Inn, Great Hampden.

Maps: OS Sheets Landranger 166; Pathfinder 1119.

An interesting walk to the west of Flaunden.

Start At: 017007, the car park at the Village Hall, Flaunden.

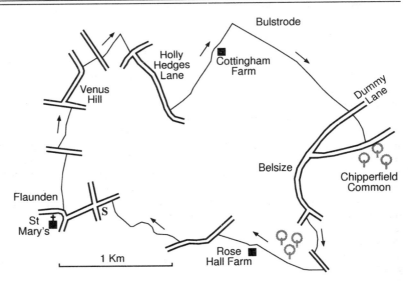

Turn right from the car park and left at the crossroads, passing Sharlowes Farm and the Green Dragon Inn. Turn right in front of **St Mary Magdalene Church** and, where the road turns left, go ahead along a fenced path to reach a lane. Turn left and, after the last house on the right, turn right along a fenced path to reach another lane. Turn left and, after passing Venus Hill dairy farm, turn right along Middle Lane. Where the road bears left, turn right over a stile. Go through farm buildings to reach Water Lane and turn right. After 15 yards, turn left over a stile. Cross two stiles and immediately turn right, with a wire fence on your right. Cross a stile at a road junction. Go ahead along Holly Hedges Lane. After 600 yards, where the lane bears left, turn left by a pair of metal gates. Go along the right field edge and through a gap to follow a grass track with a hedge on your left. Just before reaching Cottingham Farm, turn left at a marker post. After 200 yards, turn right through a gap, continuing ahead to cross a concrete track. Bear right across a field corner and, at the hedge corner, turn left towards Bulstrode. On reaching a line of trees on the left, turn right across a field, keeping left of the hedge. Go through a gap, ignore a path to the left and bear right to go over a stile. Go over another stile and along the wood edge. Chipperfield House is beyond the trees to the left. Leave the wood, maintaining direction to go through a gap. Follow a field edge and cross Dummy Lane to the stile opposite. Bear right, away from the hedge, to a stile, cross and go along a narrow path between houses. Turn right along a road, passing the Windmill Inn and following the edge of **Chipperfield Common**. Opposite the entrance to Mill House, turn left and, soon, bear right, remaining on the gravel track. At a cottage, bear right, keeping a hedge on your left. Turn left at the road into Belsize. Go past the Plough Inn and turn right into Flaunden Lane at the junction. After 500 yards, turn left over a stile (just off the road). Go over another stile, cross a lane and turn right, then immediately go left over a stile on to a gravel track. Go past Rose Hall Farm and, at the T-junction turn left, soon leaving the track and turning right. Bear right at a fork, keeping the farmhouse and stables on your right, to reach a stile. Cross and keep to the right of Great Bregmans Farm. Bear right in a paddock to reach a road. Turn left and, after 400 yards, turn right up steps and cross a stile. Bear left across the field beyond and, at the hedge corner, bear left, with Newhouse Farm on your right. Turn right at a junction and, just before the arch of trees, turn left along a fenced path. Cross a stile in the corner, bear right and cross another stile, continuing along the left edge of a field. Cross a stile and, at the lane, turn left to reach a crossroads. Turn left to return to the Village Hall.

POINTS OF INTEREST:

St Mary Magdalene Church, Flaunden – This was the first church built by the well-known builder and restorer George Gilbert Scott. He described it as 'a poor barn built for my Uncle'. Inside is a 15th-century font, some worn medieval tiles and three bells, one dated 1578, all from the old Flaunden church. This old church, only a few crumbling walls remain, can be found just east of Latimer, by the River Chess, completely hidden in a spinney.

Chipperfield Common – The Common is 100 acres of woodland surrounding a delightful cricket pitch, with inns and a first class hotel. On the Common are some huge Spanish Chestnut trees, said to have been planted for Isabel of Castile, the first Duchess of York, who lived and died in Kings Langley during the late 14th century.

REFRESHMENTS:

The Green Dragon, Flaunden.
The Windmill Inn, Chipperfield Common.
The Plough Inn, Belsize.

Maps: OS Sheets Landranger 152 and 165; Pathfinder 1046.

The undulations of the northern Aylesbury Vale.

Start: At 782343, in the High Street, Nash.

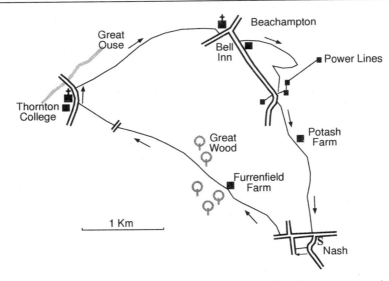

Walk northwards along the High Street and, after passing the village pump, at a right-hand bend, turn left along a signed path. Turn right along a road and left at a crossroads. Now, after 150 yards, turn right over a stile and bear left across the centre of a field. Cross a stile in a hedge and bear left and go through a hedge gap. Cross a footbridge and stile, then bear right to a stile and head for the corner of the farm buildings. Go through a metal gate, turn left across a tarmac track and go through a gate into a small paddock. Cross a stile and go through an overgrown area to reach a field. Bear right, heading for the top corner of a wood. Go across a track and, at the corner of Great Wood, go along the prominent path. Cross two stiles and a footbridge, then, as you approach the brow of this gentle climb, Thornton Hall can be seen on the left. Go through a hedge gap and cross a field corner, heading for the marker post in the top left corner. Go through a gap, cross a footbridge and bear left to cross a lane, following the track opposite, the drive to Thornton Park Farm, to a road. Turn right, with

Thornton College and church on your left. The bridge ahead, over the Great Ouse, is the boundary corner between Northamptonshire and Buckinghamshire.

Opposite the drive to the college, turn right along a signed path, bearing right, away from a wire fence. At the oak tree, take the left fork, heading towards a single telegraph pole. Cross a footbridge and stile, heading to the right of Hall Farm. Cross a stile and bear right towards the steeple of Beachampton church. Cross a stile in a fence, keeping to the left of the church to cross a stile. Bear right to a stile on to a lane. Turn left, passing **St Mary's Church**. At the T-junction, turn right passing the gates to Beachampton Place. Turn left opposite a thatched cottage, crossing a footbridge and two stiles. Bear right to a pair of stiles in the top right corner and then bear right to follow the intermittent hedge line. Cross a stile and go through a gap. Cross a stile below the electricity cables, go through a gap and immediately turn right over a stile. Turn right along farm track and, just before the ford, turn left over a stile and go along the right edge to cross a footbridge. After 80 yards, turn right over a metal gate joining a lane in the top left corner. Turn left and, after 40 yards, turn left again along a concrete drive. Bear right through a gate and follow the left field edge. Go under a double set of cables and, beyond the woodland corner, bear right to leave the hedge line. Cross a gravel track, skirting the farm buildings to cross the centre of a field. Go over a track and through a hedge gap to a stile and, beyond, a pair of stiles. Go through a metal gate, bearing left to a stile, midway along the left hedge. Turn right and go through a gate on to a farm track. Go through the farm yard to reach a road. Cross to the High Street, **Nash** and the start of the walk.

POINTS OF INTEREST:
Thornton College – Now the convent of Jesus and Mary. The original medieval Manor House was rebuilt for Richard Cavendish in 1850. The River Ouse was dammed to make an ornamental lake beside the great lawns leading to the house. The church, to St Michael, is 14th-century, but with considerable Victorian restoration.
St Mary's Church, Beachampton – Built in the 14th century but substantially restored by G E Street in 1873. Inside is a splendid monument to Simon Benet (died 1682) erected in 1960 by University College, Oxford, of whom he was a benefactor.
Nash – The village has several 16th- and 17th-century timber-framed cottages, but of particular importance is 41 High Street, Tithe Cottage, which is 15th-century with a timber frame and three cruck trusses. The National School was built in 1855. Note the remarkable staggered chimney stack on the side of the teacher's house.

REFRESHMENTS:
The Bell Inn, Beachampton.

Walk 92   **MARLOW** $6^{1}/_{2}$m (10km)

Maps: OS Sheets Landranger 175; Explorer 3.

A field walk on Marlow outskirts with a return along a stretch of Thames towpath.

Start: At 848862, the Court Gardens pay and display car park, Pound Lane, Marlow.

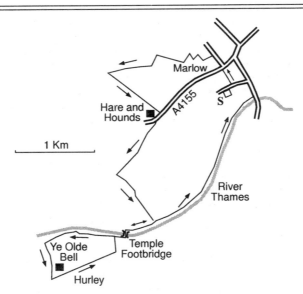

From the car park, cross the road to follow an alleyway to West Street. Turn right and, after 20 yards, left down Oxford Road. After passing the Crown and Anchor Inn and some terraced houses, turn left down an alley. Continue ahead, up some steps and cross two roads to reach Ryans Mount. Turn left and, at the iron railings, turn right along a tarmac path. Cross a road and a stile on to a fenced path, turning left into Forty Green Drive. At the junction, turn right and, after the last bungalow, turn left along a gravel footpath. Bear left by a parking area to follow the path through trees.

Soon, cross a stile on the left and walk downhill into the valley. Turn sharp left to continue along the valley path, reaching a stile under some trees. Go past some greenhouses, then go through a kissing gate and turn left along a lane to reach the main road (the A4155). Cross, with care, and turn right, along the verge. Opposite the Hare and Hounds Inn, turn left down Harleyford Lane. Go through a kissing gate and continue along a lane to reach East Lodge. Now turn left along a rough track, go through a metal gate and, at the end of the farm wall, turn right, following the lane towards the river. Turn right along the towpath, go through the lock cut and cross Temple Footbridge. Turn right to continue along the towpath, going through a gate, and crossing a stile and a footbridge to arrive at Hurley Lock Island. Walk through the lock cut and cross the footbridge. Go down the steps ahead and continue past some houses and a converted barn to reach the Historic village of **Hurley**. Go past two village shops and, just before 'Ye Olde Bell', turn left through a kissing gate. Cross a farm lane, then go past a caravan site on the left and cross a stile to join a track. Now, just before a white cottage, turn left over a stile, to return to the towpath. Turn right and recross the Temple Footbridge. Go through the lock, keeping to the towpath now for a pleasant $1^{1}/_{2}$ miles of river walking back into Marlow, passing **Bisham Abbey** and **Bisham Church** on the right. Just before the suspension bridge, turn left and, at the main park gates, turn left again down Pound Lane to return to the start.

POINTS OF INTEREST:

Hurley – The name, translated from the Saxon, means a 'bend by the river'. The 'Olde Bell Hotel was built in 1187 as the guest house for Hurley Priory. Adjacent to Hurley House in the High Street are three 17th-century almshouses in the trusteeship of Hurley Church estate. One is now the village post office. The remains of the priory, dissolved by Henry VIII in 1536, are mainly centred around the church. The large tithe barn was converted in 1950 into a private house. The well-preserved dovecote dates from the 13th century.

Bisham Abbey – Built by Philip Hoby, servant and ambassador to Henry VIII this Tudor mansion of the Renaissance period is a Grade I listed building. It is owned by the Sports Council and run as the National Sports Centre. The Abbey is said to be haunted by the repentant spirit of Elizabeth Hoby who is said to have beat her small son to death.

Bisham Church – The church is best known for its Hoby tombs, beautifully carved, gilded and coloured. The kneeling figure of Elizabeth Hoby, Lady Russell, with tight-waisted ladies and pitiful mummified rows of children, dominates the scene.

REFRESHMENTS:

There are many opportunities in Marlow and Hurley, including those mentioned in the text.

In Summer months there is an excellent tea garden by the side of Temple Lock.

Walk 93   **WADDESDON** $6^{1}/_{2}$m (10km)

Maps: OS Sheets Landranger 165; Explorer 2.

The Brill Tramway and a visit to the Bucks Railway Centre.

Start: At 743168, opposite the Five Arrows Hotel, High Street, Waddesdon.

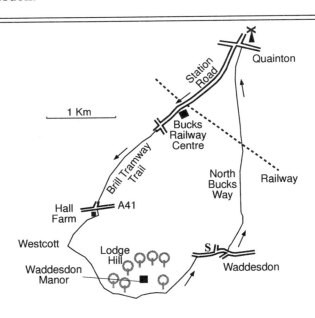

Facing the hotel, turn left down the main road and, opposite the Tyre Service garage, turn left along the North Bucks Way. At the right-hand bend, go ahead along a path to the rear of houses. Cross a stile and maintain direction over two further stiles, with Glebe Farm on your left. Cross a double stile and a footbridge and bear left to a stile to the right of the farm. Cross a track and a stile, and keep to the left edge of a field to reach a stile on the left. Cross and go through a squeeze stile on to a concrete track. Turn right, but where the track bends right, walk ahead and cross a stile into a narrow field. Bear left to the corner, with Quainton Windmill ahead. Go through a squeeze stile and over a stile on to the railway. Cross this, with care, and a series of stiles and footbridges, following the North Bucks Way waymarkers. (The farmer has a passion for electric fences – so please take care.) On reaching some houses, cross a pair of stiles and a footbridge, and follow a gravel path and a narrow alley to reach the White Hart Inn, Quainton. Turn left along the road, passing the green, the George and Dragon Inn and the windmill. Turn left along Station Road, following it for about a mile. Where the road bears right to go over the railway, turn left here if you wish to visit the Buckinghamshire Railway Centre.

The walk follows the road over the railway to reach the entrance to the **Brill Tramway Trail** car park. Take the signed tramway path, following the old tramway for nearly two miles to reach the A41. Cross, with care, bearing left to go over a stile, still following the Tramway signs. At the end of the barns of Hall Farm, turn right over a stile and go through the left-hand gate, in the corner. Cross the stile ahead and turn left, heading towards Lodge Hill. Cross two sets of stiles and footbridges and, at the top of the rise, bear left over a stile and continue with a fence on your right. Where the fence goes right, continue ahead, soon bearing left to the corner of the wood. Cross an electric fence, keeping the wooded grounds of **Waddesdon Manor** on your left. Cross a stile and a footbridge and, after 100 yards, turn left through a hedge gap into the manor grounds. The manor can be seen through the trees to the left. Turn right along a road and, at the second waymarker post, bear left, keeping to the right of the fir trees. Go through a kissing gate and over a stile. Go through another kissing gate and continue along a clear path through the trees. At the garages, join a tarmac path to reach a road. Now keep to the right of the War Memorial to regain the start.

POINT OF INTEREST:
The Brill Tramway – This started life as a horse-drawn tramway linking Quainton and Brill, but eventually became part of the London Transport network. An explanatory booklet, on which this walk is based, is available from The Recreational Paths Officer, Buckinghamshire County Council, County Hall, Aylesbury, Bucks HP20 1UY.
Waddesdon Manor – The Manor was designed by a French architect in the 1870s for Baron Ferdinand De Rothschild. The original château-like house was conceived to house the Baron's collection of furniture and art. The house was presented to the National Trust in 1957. In 1986 a substantial program of refurbishment and restoration was undertaken, this having been completed quite recently.

REFRESHMENTS:
The White Hart Inn, Quainton.
The George and Dragon, Quainton.
There are several possibilities in Waddesdon, and a café at the Railway Centre.

Maps: OS Sheets Landranger 175; Explorer 3.

Field and woodland paths south of Beaconsfield.

Start: At 944900, the Greyhound Inn, Windsor End, Beaconsfield.

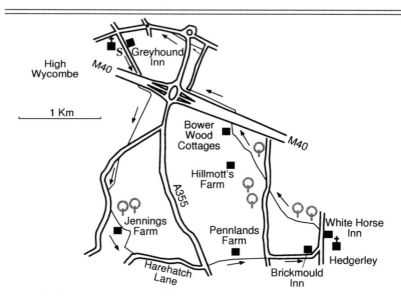

Facing the inn, turn right down Windsor End, passing Oak Lodge and crossing the motorway footbridge. Turn left along an enclosed path and, after 200 yards, go right over a stile. Bear left across a drive to cross a stile, and go through the small copse beyond. Climb steps to reach a fenced path. Go past a pond and, on leaving the wooded area, cross a track and a stile. Now, just before the field corner, cross a stile on to a road. Turn right, then, after 30 yards, left over a footbridge and go through a gate. Cross a stile in the corner and, ignoring a broad path to the left, continue ahead, downhill, to reach a road. Turn left, and take the second footpath on the left going uphill through a wood to reach Jennings Farm. Turn left along the wide track before the farm buildings and, at the 'No Footpath' sign, bear right to go through a clump of holly bushes. Cross a stile into a field, turn left, keeping the wood on your left, and cross another stile. Turn right, walking with a hedge on your right, and, in the corner, turn left, following the line of the hedge on the right. After 150 yards, cross the fence by a metal gate and turn left along Harehatch Lane, following it to reach the A355.

Cross, with care, and go along a tarmac track, passing Pennlands Kiln and Pennlands Farm, to arrive at a junction of minor lanes. Go ahead, down Kiln Lane passing some terraced cottages and soon reaching Hedgerley Village. Turn left by the Brickmould Inn, passing the White Horse Inn, with Hedgerley church behind it. After passing the Old Quaker House, go over a stile on the left and bear right towards Sutton's Wood. Bear left around the wood edge to reach a stile in the corner. Bear left to a stile in a hedge, then right, through a gap in a hedge. Now maintain direction to cross a stile on to a lane. Turn right and, almost immediately, left into a wood. At a crossing path, go ahead, crossing a stile and following a well-defined path. Go over a crossing path, then turn right along a track, and immediately left to skirt a new plantation, with Hillmott's Farm over to your left. Leave the wood, crossing a field on a marked path towards Bower Wood Cottages. Keep to their right, aiming for the motorway bridge. Cross the bridge and turn left down steps on to a fenced path. The path turns right, away from the motorway, to join a lane. Ignore the drive on the right to Hyde Farm and continue ahead, then, just before the main road, turn left over a stile and follow a path behind a wood yard. Go through a subway under the motorway link road and continue to the main road. Turn left, then go ahead at the roundabout into **Old Beaconsfield**, soon reaching **St Mary and All Saints' Church**, and the start.

POINTS OF INTEREST:

Old Beaconsfield – The old streets are lined with 15th- to 17th-century timber framed buildings, now mostly hidden behind fine, 18th-century brickwork. Old coaching inns are found in the main streets, one of which, 'The George' contains a staircase with sword cuts made by the highwayman Claude Duval whilst fighting off the Bow Street Runners.

St Mary and All Saints' Church – The church has 13th-century origins but was ruthlessly restored in 1869, having fallen into a state of disrepair, due to the then vicar living in Newgate Debtors prison and emerging only at weekends to conduct services. The result of the restoration is a large, but unexceptional church. Edmund Burke – the 18th-century essayist and statesman – who died in 1797 is buried in the nave. The tablet marking his tomb lies under a hassock in the 7th pew from the front on the south side.

REFRESHMENTS:
The Brickmould Inn, Hedgerley.
The White Horse Inn, Hedgerley.
There are many possibilities in Old Beaconsfield, including those in the text.

Maps: OS Sheets Landranger 166; Pathfinder 1096.

To the west of the historic village of Hertingfordbury, crossing the River Mimram and returning along a dismantled railway.

Start: At 306121, the White Horse Hotel, Hertingfordbury.

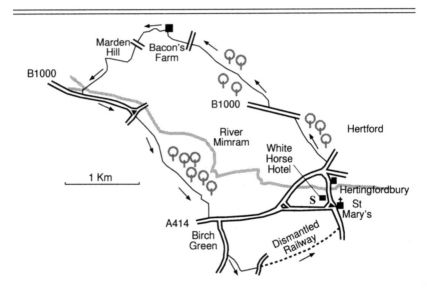

Facing the Hotel turn right, to leave **Hertingfordbury**, passing the Moat House and the Old Mill. At the roundabout, cross, with care, to go ahead along Thieves Lane. Ignore a track on the left, continuing uphill to reach a track on the right. Here, turn left through a gap into a wood. Follow the main path, emerging to cross a field corner towards Blakemore Wood. At the wood's corner, bear left passing a gravel pit on the left. Ignore a path to the right to enter a narrow section of the wood, bearing left at a fork to go through a kissing gate. Bear left across a field and go through an area of scrub to reach a road (the B1000). Turn left, crossing to the opposite, wider verge. Now, before an S-bend, turn right along a gravel track. Go past a wood on the right and follow the track around to the left. At a fork, bear left along the right field edge. Enter Selebroom Wood, emerging with the fields on your right. At the corner, go along a wide track, cross a lane and continue to Bacon's Farm. Bear left, with the farm buildings on your right and, at the hedge, bear left to follow it, keeping Red Wood on your left. Cross a road and go along a tarmac track signed for Marden Hill. At a fork, with houses on the right, bear left and pass Marden Hill House. Go over a stile and bear right, with the grounds of the house on your right. Follow a fence around to pass the side elevation of the house. Leave the fence and go ahead to reach a stile in the corner. Turn left and, soon, bear right to a lane. Cross an old bridge over the River Mimram and, at the B1000, turn left for about $^1/_2$ mile ignoring paths both right and left. Bear right at a fork, and go ahead at a T-junction. Go over a stile to the left of Poplars Green Lodge and bear right along a wide grass track (Path No. 10), initially following the line of the electricity cables. On reaching a gravel track, turn right to cross a stile. Keep to the right edge to reach another stile, then go uphill along the edge of a new plantation. At a T-junction, turn right along the wood's edge. Cross a footbridge on to a tarmac path and turn right at the end of the new plantation. Go through an area of scrub, turn left, and then right to cross a stile. Continue ahead, following a track beside cottages to reach the A414. Turn left and soon right, with care, along a road for Birch Green. Ignore paths on either side to reach a right-hand bend. There, take the cul-de-sac on the left and follow a path between houses. Cross a stile on to a dismantled railway. Turn left and, soon, go up steps to cross a road. Continue along **Cole Green Way** to reach a bridge over St Mary's Lane. Cross and turn right, down steps, on to a road. Turn right to return to Hertingfordbury, passing St Mary's Church.

POINTS OF INTEREST:

Hertingfordbury – This village on the River Mimram was originally a Saxon settlement. It was designated a conservation area in 1968. The Moat House was built in the early 19th century. The White Horse Hotel, originally a 16th-century house with a Georgian brick facade, has been an inn for many years. It was recently acquired by Trust House Forte, and enlarged as a Heritage Hotel. St Mary's Church is 13th-century, but extensively restored in 1890 by the 7th Earl and Countess Cowper of Penhanger, who added the memorial chapel with its monuments to the Cowper family. **Cole Green Way** – This popular walk along the disused railway line is managed by the Hertfordshire County Council and follows the route of the Welwyn - Hertford branch line which opened in 1858 and closed in 1966. The scrub land has been allowed to develop on either side of the path, providing an ideal habitat for wildlife.

REFRESHMENTS:
The White Horse Hotel, Hertingfordbury.
The Prince of Wales, Hertingfordbury.

Walk 96   AYOT ST LAWRENCE $6^1/_2$m (10km)

Maps: OS Sheets Landranger 166; Pathfinder 1095 and 1096.

Along the Lea Valley south of Ayot St Lawrence.

Start At: 195168, the remains of the church, Ayot St Lawrence.

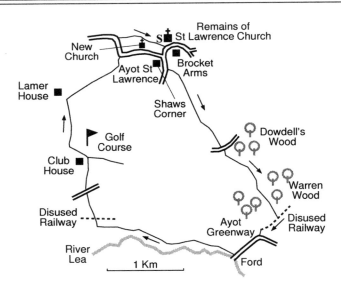

Facing the church, turn left down the lane passing **Shaws Corner**. Continue downhill and, at the S-bend, turn left along a bridleway. Follow this well-defined track between hedges and fences for about a mile to reach a lane. Cross and follow the bridleway opposite along the left edge of Dowdell's Wood. Ignore a path to the right, continuing along the wood edge. Go over a crossing track, maintaining direction between Bladder Wood and Warren Wood. Now, just before Hunters railway bridge, turn right up steps, to join a wide track, the Ayot Greenway, along the disused railway line. Turn right and, after a few hundred yards, turn left up steps at Waterend Ford, soon reaching Waterend Lane. Turn right, following the lane downhill. Before the ford, opposite a fine red-brick house, turn right along a bridleway. Ignore a path to the right, continuing along the wide track with the River Lea on your left. At a fork, bear left, remaining on a wide track close to the river. Go through a gap in a hedge, following the Lea Valley

Walk waymarkers. The path narrows and follows a hedge on the left: go through a kissing gate and continue ahead. After passing a wooden seat, bear right into a field corner and go through a kissing gate. Turn left to rejoin the wide bridleway. The town of Wheathamstead can be seen on the left.

Go through a gate and turn right along a gravel track. After 100 yards, turn left up the slope to reach a gap in the hedge – difficult to see and not waymarked – to cut across the corner of the field. Cross the disused railway line and, before the track sweeps to the right, turn right up a slope to cross a stile. Leave a small wood and cross a road. Walk beside the drive to Lamer Wood Country Club and Golf Course and, before the clubhouse, on the left, cross the drive, maintaining direction and then turning left at the T-junction. Keep the car park on your left, continuing ahead along a track into the wood. Where the wide track ends, bear right through a swing gate and turn right along a gravel track. Ignore a stile to the left, continuing to reaching Lamer House. Go ahead along a tarmac drive, then bear right at the three-way fork in front of Lamer Park Farm to reach a stile. The wide, fenced track beyond runs between mature trees. Cross a stile and, at a fork, keep left, going through the trees to reach a lane. Turn left and, after 300 yards, at a sharp left-hand bend, turn right through a gap and go along a fenced path. Cross three stiles, continuing with trees to your right, to cross another stile. Go through the churchyard gates of the new **St Lawrence's Church** and, at the T-junction, turn left. Now before the end of the drive, turn left through a kissing gate and go through a gate on to a temporary fenced path. Go through a gate and, at the lane, turn left to return to the old church and the **Brocket Arms**.

POINTS OF INTEREST:

Shaws Corner – This early 20th-century house, built as the New Rectory, was the home of George Bernard Shaw from 1906 until his death in 1950. The rooms remain as in his lifetime, with many literary and personal relics. In the garden is the summer house where he was able to work uninterrupted. The house is now owned by the National Trust and is open from April to October, Wednesday to Sunday afternoons.

St Lawrence's Church – This 14th-century church was destroyed on the orders of Sir Lionel Lyde because it spoiled the view from Ayot House, his new home. Total demolition was stopped by the Bishop of Lincoln. The new church (said to have been modelled on the Temple of Apollo at Delos) was built in 1778 by Nicholas Revett.

Brocket Arms – The inn was built in the 14th century, but greatly restored in the 17th century. The name is from a Lord of the Manor, Lord Brocket of nearby Brocket Hall.

REFRESHMENTS:

The Brocket Arms, Ayot St Lawrence.

Walk 97   CUBLINGTON   7m (11km)

Maps: OS Sheets Landranger 165; Pathfinder 1071.

History all the way on this lengthy walk.

Start At: 838222, Cublington Church.

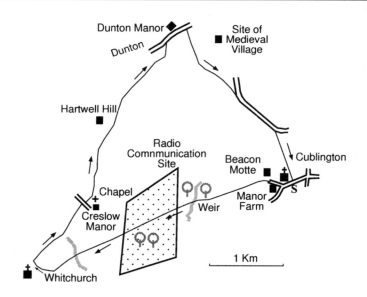

Parking is available in the Unicorn Inn car park, or in adjacent streets. If you use the inn car park please ask the landlord's permission. Facing the church, turn left and bear right down Ridings Way. Go past Manor Farm, continuing downhill along a rough track. Keep left of a cottage and cross a stile, bearing left across the field beyond. Go past the earthworks – **Beacon Motte** – on the right, and the site of a medieval village on the left beyond the pond. Cross a stile by a pair of gates and follow a well-defined path to cross a footbridge. Bear left, heading between the radio communication buildings and a clump of trees. Cross two stiles, maintaining direction through the radio site. Soon the tower of Whitchurch church can be seen ahead. Leave the radio complex over a stile, cross a small paddock and a pair of stiles, following the wire fence on the left. Go through a gate and cross a footbridge, bearing away from the left field edge. Ignore a path on the left and cross a stile to the right of the field corner. Turn right, then bear left through a gate, heading for the fence corner. There, turn right and, after 80 yards, turn right over a stile and follow the right edge of a field. Go through two sets of gates, cross a stile in the top right corner and go uphill to reach a pair of gates. Go through, bear right and skirt a pond to reach a pair of gates. Go through, cross the tarmac track and go over a stile, passing, on your right, the original chapel to **Creslow Manor**.

Bear away from the stone wall and go through double gates. Bear left to a double stile and a footbridge, cross and head now for a gap in the top right corner. Go through a gate, following the uphill path to another gate. Cross a double stile and a ladder stile and continue along a narrow path. Turn right along a tarmac drive to reach the road in Dunton. Turn right, passing **St Martin's Church** on the left. Turn right along a footpath, beside the Old Rectory, go through a gap in the corner and continue with a hedge on your right. Cross the centre of a field and go through a gap at the top of the hill. To the left, just to the right of Littlecote Farm, are the remains of the medieval village of Lidcote. Go through two gaps to cross a ditch, then over three stiles to reach a lane. Turn right, cross a stream and continue along the lane for $\frac{1}{2}$ mile. Go past some farm buildings and, after a further 150 yards, turn right along a marked path. Go through a wooden gate and cross a field corner to the stile opposite, heading for Cublington Church. Cross a series of stiles, maintaining direction towards the church and, on nearing it, cross the last stile between the thatched cottages. Keep to the right of the cottages to reach the road and the start of the walk.

POINTS OF INTEREST:

Beacon Motte – The motte of a Norman castle lies 500 yards west of the church, together with earthworks of an earlier village and church. The present church of St Nicholas marks the rejuvenation of the village.

Creslow Manor – Some early 14th-century parts of the manor remain, but the house was altered in about 1600 and added to in the 19th and 20th centuries. The parish church is now a farm building. The north door has reused parts of a Norman arch, and the roof is 15th-century, with tie beams, arch beams and wind braces.

St Martin's Church, Dunton – The nave is 12th-century, the chancel 13th-century and the tower 15th-century. The church was substantially rebuilt in 1790 and retains its 18th-century box pews and pulpit.

REFRESHMENTS:
The Unicorn, Cublington.

Maps: OS Sheets Landranger 165; Explorer 2.

Towpath walk along a stretch of the Grand Union canal, with a
circular section through the villages of Hulcott and Bierton.
Start At: 823134, the Walton Street car park, Aylesbury.

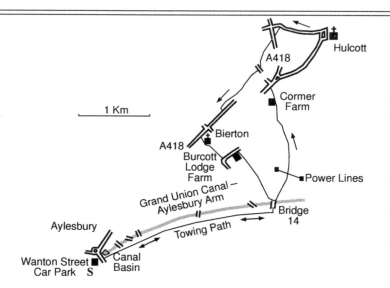

Turn right by the Ship Inn and join the towpath on the right. Follow the towpath for
$1^1/_2$ miles, going under or around six bridges and three locks. Cross a stile in front of
bridge No. 14 and go over the canal. Cross a footbridge and stile and bear left through
a gate to continue ahead. The next stile is between the two nearest electricity pylons.
Cross a field, passing an electricity sub-station on the left. Cross a stile and a footbridge
to reach a marker post, maintaining direction across a narrow field. Go through a gap
in the hedge, and continue to the gap opposite. Turn left. Do not cross the stile in the
corner: instead, turn right to walk with a hedge on the left. Cross a stile and immediately
turn right over another stile. Go left along the field edge, through a kissing gate and
between the bungalow and the farm buildings to reach a farm track. Turn left, passing
a bungalow, on the left, and bearing right towards a road. Just before reaching the
road, turn right, following the lane past a de-restriction sign. Turn right at a T-junction,

passing a golf driving range. Follow the lane into the attractive village of Hulcott. Go past Church Farm, on the left, and bear right across the Village Green. Go past the School House, on the left, with its interesting chimney formation and bell turret, and All Saints' Church on the right. A short detour behind the church enables you to view a clearly defined moated site in front of Manor Farm. The walk turns left at the top of the Green, passing the green triangle and going down a lane. Go past the drive to Cane End Farm and, after 200 yards, before a left bend, turn left over a stile. The stile is set back from the road, by a willow tree, and is difficult to see. At a hedge corner go ahead, crossing two stiles in the corner. Cross the A418, with care, to a stile. Cross and bear to the left of a brick stable. Cross a stile and head to the right of the cottages. Cross two stiles to join a lane. Go basically ahead to cross a stile, and bear left through a gate to the left of the top corner. Bear right across a field corner to a stile. Cross and follow a well-defined path crossing a series of stiles and a track. Continue along a narrow path, then cross two stiles and follow a concrete path. Turn left and, at the A418, turn right into **Bierton**. Go past the Red Lion Inn (over 500 years old) and St James the Great Church, then cross the road, with care, and turn left down a gravel drive to a stile by a gate. Keep to the left field edge to go through a gap. Cross a stile in a clump of trees and bear left to a lane. Turn left and, immediately after passing Burcott Lodge Farm, turn right over a stile and go along the right field edge. After 150 yards, turn right over a stile and then left through a narrow field. Cross a stile, a track and another stile, and go along the left edge. Cross two stiles and bear left between ponds to a stile by the canal bridge. Cross the bridge, turn right, and then left along the towpath, retracing your steps to the **Aylesbury Arm** canal basin.

POINTS OF INTEREST:

Aylesbury Arm – Opened in 1814 the Arm linked Aylesbury with the Grand Union Canal at Startop's End near Marsworth. The canal rises 94 feet 8 inches using a total of 16 locks. The canal buildings at the Aylesbury basin were once very extensive but all have gone now except the Ship Inn and a small warehouse. The canal survived commercially until the 1950s despite competition from the now dismantled railway. **Bierton** – The Vicarage Garden Iron Age site has yielded evidence of intensive occupation. The outlines of numerous ditched enclosures and circular buildings with grain storage pits have been found. Luxury goods have also been discovered, such as Roman pottery made in Gaul before the Roman conquest of Britain.

REFRESHMENTS:
The Ship Inn, Aylesbury Canal Basin.
The Red Lion, Bierton.

CHESS VALLEY

Maps: OS Sheets Landranger 165 and 166; Explorer 2 and 3; Pathfinder 1139.

A linear walk by the River Chess, returning from Chorleywood.
Start: 961016, the public car park at Chesham Station.

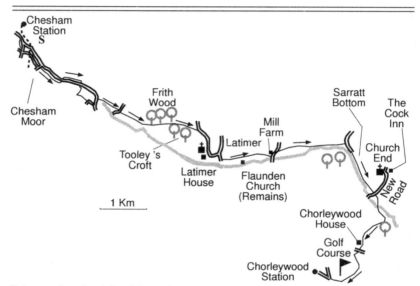

Take a path to the right of the station, passing steps and turning right down a slope to a road. Cross and go through Meades Water Gardens to rejoin the road. Turn left down Moor Road. Go under the railway and follow a path by the river. At a footbridge turn right, then, by a swimming pool, turn left, cross the road and go along a footpath on to Chesham Moor. At a crossing path, cross the river and maintain direction. Turn right over a footbridge and follow a fenced path skirting industrial units. Go through a kissing gate and turn left along a field edge. Cross a stile and follow a narrow path to a road. After 200 yards, turn left along a road, cross the river and, almost immediately, turn right, uphill. After a few yards, turn right over a stile and follow the right edge, on the higher level. Cross a pair of stiles, then bear left, uphill. Cross two stiles, following the wall of Blackwell Hall. Go right to join a lane, turn left and, after a few yards, turn right along a track. Bear right through a gate and, after the barns, take the second fork right, over a stile. Go through three gates, then bear left, uphill along a wood edge. Bear right on leaving the wood and left of the wood corner, crossing two stiles to a road. Walk ahead, downhill, passing Latimer House and St Mary Magdalene Church. Beyond the church, turn left and go through two gates to **Latimer Village Green**. Leave the Green, turn right and, after 100 yards, turn left, over a stile and bear left, with the river on your right. At the first stile, the remains of Flaunden Church can be seen on the right. Pass the **Liberty Brick Tomb** and continue to Mill Farm. Go through the yard and turn left along a lane. After 100 yards, turn right along the top of a bank. Cross several stiles and go through a small woodland, joining the river on the right. At a concrete track, walk ahead, with watercress beds on your right. At a T-junction by white cottages, turn right and, where the lane bends left, go ahead. Cross two stiles and go down a rough track. Cross New Road (turn left here for the Cock Inn) and go along the right field edge. Turn right into a small copse, cross a footbridge and turn left through a gate. Take the right fork and, at a T-junction, turn right over a stile signed for Chorleywood Station. Follow the path uphill through trees to a minor lane. Turn left, uphill, with Chorleywood House on your right. Cross a road, go through the parking area and bear right along a grass track. After 500 yards, before an open area, turn left, go over two crossing paths and cross a golf course. Cross the last of the fairways, turn right along a track, following it around to the left, go through a parking area and turn right. Take the left fork, with the station car park now ahead. To return take the train to Chesham, changing at Chalfont and Latimer.

POINTS OF INTEREST:

Latimer Village Green – Two monuments can be found on the village green. The first is dedicated to the men of the village who died in the Boer War. Beside it is a stone mound bearing a plaque in memory of a horse. The horse was ridden by a General, the local squire, at the battle of Boshof, South Africa, on 5th April 1900. The General was killed and the horse wounded. The horse was brought to England later that year and died in 1911. The horses' heart, ceremonial trappings and harness are buried under the puddingstone memorial.

Liberty Tomb – This brick tomb marks the resting place of William Liberty, who died in 1777. He was a relative of the family of Liberty's of Regent Street. The tomb also contains the remains of Alice Liberty, his wife, who died in 1809.

REFRESHMENTS:

The Cock Inn, just off the route in Church End.

The farm shop at Mill Farm is open seven days a week selling ice cream and snacks. There are also plenty of opportunities in Chesham and Chorleywood.

Walk 100   KINGS LANGLEY   10m (16km)

Maps: OS Sheets Landranger 166; Pathfinder 1119.

A walk of contrasts: field and woodland paths, ancient lanes and a return along the Grand Union Canal.

Start: At 072026, the free car park, Langley Hill, Kings Langley.

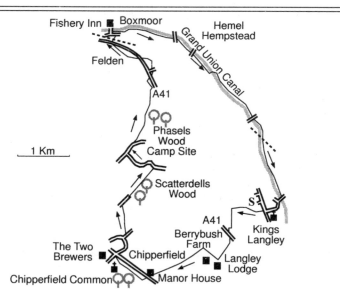

The car park is just off the High Street, opposite the Saracen's Head Inn. Return to the High Street, turn right, and, opposite All Saints' Church, turn right beside the Rose and Crown Inn. Follow a tarmac path, cross the road and, after 40 yards, bear right, continuing uphill. Go over a crossing path and, near the top, turn left over a stile. Cross the centre of the field beyond, then cross a pair of stiles and turn right. Bear left and cross a footbridge over the A41. Bear left to cross two stiles, then follow a well-defined path, with a hedge on your left. Cross two stiles and go through a small copse to reach a track. Turn right in front of Berrybush Farm. Bear right along a wide track between hedges and, at a T-junction, turn left over a stile. Cross another stile and follow the track downhill and through a gate. Before the corner, cross a stile, go through the bushes and continue along the right field edge. Maintain direction across seven stiles to reach a road. Take the path opposite on to Chipperfield Common. After 30 yards, turn right along a bridleway. The **Manor House** is across the road to the right. Emerge from the wooded area and head for the **Two Brewers Hotel**. At the crossroads, turn right along Kings Lane, following it to a T-junction. Turn right, and then left along a path beside a bus shelter. Ignore paths joining from the left to reach a tarmac lane. Turn right and go over a stile into Scatterdells Wood. Follow a wide path, bear right at a fork, then right again at the next fork. At a T-junction, turn right and, after 80 yards, turn left, uphill. At the top, turn left along the wood edge. Before reaching the corner, turn right over a stile. Bear right, half-way across the field, to a stile on to a lane. Turn left, and follow the lane to its T-junction with Rucklers Lane. Turn right and, at the right-hand bend, turn left along a wide bridle way. Pass the Phasels Wood camping site and reach a road by the A41. Turn left and, at a left-hand bend, go right through a swing gate, down steps and under the A41. Cross the slip road exit and immediately turn left through a gate. Go through two gates towards Felden. In the corner, go through two gates, bearing left along a path. Cross a stile and turn right to cross a bridge. Ignore the steps on the left, going downhill and through a kissing gate. Turn right along a crossing path, going downhill and through a gate. Go along a fenced path. Now do not go under the main road: instead, turn left along a fenced path and, at its end, go under the A41, cross a road and go under two railway bridges. Bear left along a tarmac path towards the Fishery Inn. Go down steps before a bridge and turn right under the road to follow the towpath. Follow the towpath for 3 miles to return to Kings Langley, crossing the canal where necessary. (Cross the bridge at the end of the **Paper Works** and do not follow the path ahead.) After Lock 69a, bear left to leave the towpath. Cross the canal bridge and, at the junction with Waterside, by the general store, turn right. Soon, by No. 19a, turn left along a tarmac path, following it to the High Street.

POINTS OF INTEREST:
Manor House – Originally known as Pynglesgate House, the Manor is a late 16th-century medieval hall house.
Two Brewers Hotel – Originally the inn boasted a large gymnasium used for the training of leading boxers. Bob Fitzsimmons is said to have trained here.
John Dickinson's Paper Works – Several canal side mills were operated by John Dickinson. Both Nash and Apsley mills were originally corn mills converted to paper mills at the end of the 18th century.

REFRESHMENTS:
Those mentioned in the text, as well as several other possibilities in Kings Langley.

TITLES IN THE SERIES